■

Dedicated

to

SAM

PECKINPAH

and

ANDREI

TARKOVSKY

■

THE 100 BEST FILMS TO RENT YOU'VE NEVER HEARD OF

St. Martin's Griffin

New York

"*Obviously, if you combine style and content, you have the best of all possible films.*"
—STANLEY KUBRICK

Hidden Treasures, Neglected Classics, and Hits from Bygone Eras

THE
100
BEST
FILMS
TO
RENT
YOU'VE
NEVER
HEARD
OF

DAVID N. MEYER

All photos reprinted by permission from Archive Photos.

Design by Songhee Kim

Library of Congress Cataloging-in-Publication Data

Meyer, David N.
      The 100 best films to rent you've never heard of :   hidden
treasures, neglected classics, and hits from bygone eras   /   David
N. Meyer
          p.   cm.
      ISBN 0-312-15042-3
      1. Motion pictures—Catalogs.   2. Video recordings—Catalogs.
I. Title
PN1998.M358   1997
216.79143'75—dc20   96-32865
                                                            CIP

10   9   8   7   6   5   4   3

■ ■ ■

In the hands of a free spirit the cinema is a magnificent and dangerous weapon. It is the superlative medium through which to express the world of thought, feeling, and instinct.

A film is like an involuntary imitation of a dream. The darkness that slowly settles over a movie theater is equivalent to the act of closing the eyes. Then, on the screen, as within a human being, the nocturnal voyage into the unconscious begins.

The device of fading allows images to appear and disappear as in a dream; time and space become flexible, shrinking and expanding at will; chronological order and the relative values of time duration no longer correspond to reality; cyclical action can last a few minutes or several centuries; shifts from slow motion to accelerated action heighten the impact of each.

The cinema seems to have been invented to express the life of the subconscious, the roots of which penetrate poetry so deeply.

—LUIS BUÑUEL

CONTENTS

INTRODUCTION

■ This book is your guide to the seldom-visited back shelves of your video-rental outlet, where *The 100 Best Films to Rent You've Never Heard Of* await.

Think of all the times you've stood in the New Releases section, scratching your head, flummoxed by the ever-changing collection of the same old stuff. Or every time you asked that Tarantino wannabe behind the counter to recommend "something good," and went home with *Last Year at Marienbad, I Am Curious (Yellow),* or *Howard the Duck.*

Never mind the latest thing; it's probably terrible. Hidden on the shelves surrounding you—and this is true of even the most rural and desolate convenience stores—are great movies you've never heard of. Or classics you've never seen. Or wonderful pictures by prominent directors that weren't properly appreciated at the time of their release. Surrounding you in that video store is the entire history of cinema in all its glory. If only you knew where to look . . .

This book offers suggestions for all sorts of films: westerns, comedies, drama, horror, sci-fi, romance, date movies, war movies, art movies, foreign movies, documentaries, rock 'n' roll movies, and classics. Each film is a success on its own terms and—regardless of when it was produced—fun to watch. Every pure entertainment chosen for this book can make a claim to art; every art film included is entertaining. No film in this book was chosen for its obscurity.

Each review is designed to present the atmosphere of the film for those who haven't seen it, and to offer illumination for those who have. Included is just enough of a plot summary to help you decide whether to rent it.

Because we so often rent to suit our mood, each review begins with a Mood Guide©. One glance and you'll know whether to rent a Technicolor action extravaganza (*The Adventures of Robin Hood*), a French sci-fi quest (*Le Dernier Combat*), a profound suspense thriller (*Out of the Past*), or an arty mind-blowing adventure (*Aguirre, the Wrath of God*).

When you find a favorite among these little-known gems, note the director, the cinematographer, or the screenwriter and search out their other films. To assist you, every review offers a comprehensive list of other worthy film rentals by the same director or concerning the same subject matter.

I learned to love movies during what is now considered the last Golden Age of Cinema: the early 1970s. The film artists that shaped my taste—Peckinpah, Altman, Godard, Herzog, Wenders, Hopper, Scorsese, Antonioni, and others—all worked in an arena of freedom and experimentation that today's blockbuster-oriented marketplace forbids.

What those who mourn this Golden Age forget, however, is how difficult it was to *see* these films in the first place. If you weren't a film student, or didn't live in a big city, forget it. That was a time of groundbreaking cinema, but the best time to be a film student or movie lover is right now. With little effort, we can explore any genre, any director's body of work, any subject that intrigues us.

In the Golden Age, the cineast's problem was Not Enough; today's problem is Too Many. Too many new releases, too many films to choose from, too many titles. This book will help you cut through the clutter. It will guide you to a choice, a hundred choices, and every choice is designed to lead you to even more wonderful pictures.

If you wonder by what criteria I chose these films, the answer is simple: I chose them because I think they're great, and because they never got the attention they deserved. Or, in the case of most of the classics—such as *Red River, The Lady Eve, Black Narcissus,* or *The Adventures of Robin Hood*—because, outside of the world of film schools, these historic pictures no longer earn the awe they deserve. I've watched every one of these films numerous times and find they all reward repeat viewings just as they enchant the first time around.

And by the time you've rented all *100 Best Films,* I should be working on the sequel. If I've omitted any of your favorites, please E-mail your comments or suggestions to: 100films@aol.com.

How to Use This Book

Homicide

Existential cops & self-discovery[1] **:ATTITUDE**
Intellectual cop movie[2] **:MOOD**

DIRECTOR: David Mamet (1990—U.S.A.)[3]
CAST: Joe Mantegna, William H. Macy, Ving Rhames[4]
IN ENGLISH; COLOR[5]

Title (Arranged alphabetically)
1. **ATTITUDE:** A summary of a film's content, of its attitude toward itself, of the reviewer's attitude toward the film, or all three combined.
2. **MOOD:** Match your mood to the mood of the film you want to rent. If you combine the Attitude Guide and the Mood Guide, a clear picture of your likely viewing experience should emerge.
3. **DIRECTOR:** Also includes year of commercial release and nation of origin (or of cofinancing).
4. **CAST:** Principal cast members.
5. The language of the film's dialogue; whether it was shot in color or in black-and-white (B/W).

All 100 films have been comprehensively indexed. By turning to the back of the book, you can search for films by actor, director, or by rental category. These categories were chosen to match the filing system at most video-rental outlets and include: Action, Classic, Comedy, Costume, Documentary, Drama, Foreign, Horror, Rock 'n' Roll, Sci-Fi, Shakespeare, Thriller, War, and Westerns.

THE
100
BEST
FILMS
TO
RENT
YOU'VE
NEVER
HEARD
OF

The Adventures of Robin Hood

Heartfelt swashbuckling **:ATTITUDE**
Self-amused Technicolor action extravaganza **:MOOD**

DIRECTOR: Michael Curtiz (1938—U.S.A.)
CAST: Errol Flynn, Claude Rains, Olivia de Havilland, Basil Rathbone
IN ENGLISH; TECHNICOLOR

Basil Rathbone and Errol Flynn in *The Adventures of Robin Hood*

They don't make 'em like this anymore. Really, they never did. The
witty dialogue, the exquisite costumes, the brazen simplicity of the
plot . . .

Errol Flynn's pleasure in his own physical exuberance makes him
the quintessential Robin Hood. He's lighthearted and amiable with
no diminishment of star power, playing himself with total confidence.
Flynn's readiness to jump out of trees, leap onto horses, swing across
rooms on chandeliers, and sword-fight like a demon forms the core
of this film's fun.

Robin Hood's enemies are the essence of urbane, articulate evil. Claude Rains and Basil Rathbone mock one another with courtly barbs while clad in an eye-popping array of lustrous colors—colors made possible by the irreplaceable three-step Technicolor process. Older Technicolor films shot in the original three-strip process capture hues that the modern two-step process cannot, particularly in shades of green and blue.

The pacing is swift and clean. There are no lags, not a single dull conversation, and the editing is surprisingly modern. Unlike many films of this era, there are few repetitive cuts to close-ups, and each cut informs the characters. And these characters are presented with all the richness of the original mythology. This isn't some cookie-cutter modern actioner where only the hero and villain possess depth and everybody else is cardboard.

The only lapse into the corniness symbolic of this bygone era occurs when Robin throws his chin into the air and laughs—"Ah-ha-ha-ha-ha . . . "—with every tooth in his head agleam. However preposterous, the guy still charms.

The climactic sword-fight between Robin and Guy of Guisbane (Basil Rathbone at his hangdog, lugubrious best) goes on and on, moving across a castle, up a flight of stairs, and even into the land of shadows, with never an unimaginative moment. The only film with similarly superb fight choreography is Richard Lester's *The Three Musketeers* (1974).

This rollicking big-studio, big-budget diversion should never be confused with the noisy, turgid melodramas Hollywood rolls out today. It belongs to the era of easygoing, self-amused, literate extravaganzas like *The Four Feathers* or *Gunga Din*. It's a different kind of good time for kids and a deeply satisfying wonderland for adults.

One dated and glaring flaw: The singing Will Scarlet is, it must be admitted, unbearable—fey, dressed like a circus clown, cloying and annoying. But he's only one guy in a cast of hundreds.

Aguirre, the Wrath of God

Existential conquistadors :**ATTITUDE**

Arty mind-blowing travelogue/adventure :**MOOD**

DIRECTOR: Werner Herzog (1972—Germany)
CAST: Klaus Kinski, Cecilia Rivera
IN GERMAN WITH ENGLISH SUBTITLES; COLOR

For a while in the late 1970s/early 1980s, Werner Herzog wore the mantle of Greatest Director in the World, and this is his finest hour. Klaus Kinski stars as the megalomaniacal conquistador Aguirre, who leads his men into the wildest, most inaccessible reaches of the Amazonian wilderness in search of gold. Based on the true story of a renegade conquistador who defied Spanish authority to claim a kingdom of his own, *Aguirre* boldly went where no other movie ever dared to tread.

Herzog took his shoestring crew and cast out into the jungle on a labor of love, determination, and artistic vision and made them stay until they got it right. There is not one interior shot in the film. Everything is shot outdoors, on location, at who-knows-what-cost in human ingenuity, forbearance, and life expectancy. Herzog, famous for megalomania, is rumored to have dealt with Klaus Kinski's desire to flee the jungle—and the picture—by brandishing a pistol and offering to kill Kinski if he tried to escape.

Kinski, equally famous for his tantrums and diva high-handedness, elected to stick around. Having effectively handled labor strife, Herzog sent his players onto crude rafts in the middle of the Amazon, forced them to climb high Andean passes in costume, and fired stunt arrows into their (barely) padded chests. Through these extremes he achieves jaw-dropping realism. Herzog's hyperrealism is often too real to absorb; his images seem to turn into dreams.

However hard such a shoot might have been on the production company, it achieved results. The cinematography is overwhelming, not only for the beauty of the images, but also because they appear so impossibly difficult to attain. Herzog went into the jungle seeking poetry. Unlike so many others who claim to find their muse in adversity, he came back with a masterpiece.

The tale moves slowly. Aguirre goes insane, murders the Spanish lord in charge, and leads his dwindling army deeper and deeper into the Amazon. The conquistadors slide down the river, claiming all they see in the name of Spain. The Spaniards fear the Indians and they fear demons, but they fear Aguirre the most, and for good reason.

Deep in the outback, European culture dissolves: Indians attack, rivers rise, the veneer of civilization cracks. Only the strong survive and nobody's stronger than Aguirre. Don't forget: His nickname is "The Wrath of God." There's little dialogue, and who needs it? Herzog makes it clear that the Spaniards fall prey to the inexorable—and spiritually superior—primitive forces surrounding them. Yes, it's the territory of *Apocalypse Now* (or even *Hearts of Darkness*), but Herzog's commitment and vision put his work on a par with either.

What this German mystic and his films lack is a conventional sense of narrative. Herzog makes time pile up like an L.A. rush hour. No director can make fifteen minutes crawl by so slowly, and no other can create a lifetime of memories with a single shot.

A picture to be in the mood for: a patient mood, arty and ready to be astounded. If you're up for it, this is a film you will not forget, a basis of comparison to which few measure up.

Other recommended rentals directed by Werner Herzog:
Every Man for Himself and God Against All (aka **The Mystery of Kaspar Hauser**)
Fata Morgana
Nosferatu
Stroszek

The American Friend

Arty noir :**ATTITUDE**
Hypnotic, compelling suspense :**MOOD**

DIRECTOR: Wim Wenders (1977—Germany)
CAST: Dennis Hopper, Nicholas Ray, Bruno Ganz, Samuel Fuller
IN ENGLISH AND SOME GERMAN WITH ENGLISH SUBTITLES; COLOR

Wim Wenders's best movies are astonishing hybrids of American energy and European artiness. That's no easy trick: When Wenders indulges his arty side the results can be torturously slow. Here, for the only time in his career, Wenders renounces self-consciousness and devotes himself to plot, character, cinematography, and suspense. The result is a modern cinematic landmark.

On the one hand is Ripley (Dennis Hopper): a speed freak, a hustler, a stylish, rootless moneymaker with the attention span of a gnat, the arrogance of a vampire, and the aggressive instincts of a wolverine. On the other, Jonathan (Bruno Ganz): self-contained, stolid, an old-world craftsman, the good burgher whose safe universe contains his craft, his family, and the denial of everything else. Ripley confronts his dread by laying waste to whatever appears in his path. Jonathan hides from the certain knowledge of his own mortality by creating objects that endure. The two collide, and the tale is launched.

In Wenders's adaptation of Patricia Highsmith's dark suspense novel *Ripley's Game,* Ganz and Hopper run the roundelay of adult male friendship: suspicion, insult, revenge, grudging admiration, teamwork, and, in the end, betrayal. Hopper gives the performance of his life. Wenders cast Hopper at the absolute bottom of his career, when Hopper was regarded as not merely drug-addled and unhirable, but genuinely psychotic. Hopper's spontaneous, instinctive acting was as much an irritant to the controlled, overrehearsed Ganz as Hopper's character Ripley is to Ganz's Jonathan.

A famous, drunken fistfight between Hopper and Ganz midway through shooting smoothed things between them and mirrored offscreen the uneasy alliance forming between their characters.

To showcase this clash between the archetypal American and the ultimate European, Wenders successfully invented a new genre: the intersection of European art film and American noir. The hypnotic pace, solemn camera work, and unshakable air of profundity—plus a slew of famous film directors in cameo appearances—equals Art Film with a capital A. The extraordinary suspense, unbearable tension, understated violence, and inescapable existential doom are hallmarks of *noir.*

Though the plot may not make a whole lot of sense the first time around—and the thick European accents of a couple of the major actors don't help—*The American Friend* is worth the effort. Few movies from any era or genre offer such rich characters, realistic human relationships, gripping action sequences, or sly humor.

Check out the gleeful, sadistic cameo by American director—and

Wenders mentor—Nicholas Ray (*Rebel Without a Cause, In a Lonely Place*), and the controlled moral rage of Lisa Kruezer, Wenders's wife at the time of filming. Add to this the deep, oversaturated colors, the perfect and perfectly weird supporting cast, and the astounding music of Bernard Herrmann—he scored most of Hitchcock's films—and the result is a film you will rent again and again, and discover new pleasures in every time.

Other recommended rentals directed by Wim Wenders:

Alice in the Cities
Paris, Texas
State of Things (see page 160)
Wings of Desire

At Close Range

Oedipal farmland noir **:ATTITUDE**
Scary psychological action/drama **:MOOD**

DIRECTOR: James Foley (1985—U.S.A.)
CAST: Sean Penn, Christopher Walken, Mary Stuart Masterson
IN ENGLISH; COLOR

Based on the true story of a contemporary father-son gang of thieves, and of the father's betrayal of the son, this modern noir brings all the existential dread usually associated with rain-slicked nighttime city streets to the sunny farmlands of Pennsylvania.

Sean Penn's adolescent aimlessness has no criminal component until he reunites with the father who abandoned him, played to cunning, redneck perfection by Christopher Walken. Hoping to earn his dad's love, Penn becomes embroiled in his father's gang of tractor thieves. When Sean tries to leave the gang behind, he learns a hard lesson about the limits of paternal forgiveness.

Before Walken's much-deserved success turned his diabolical menace into self-parody, he brought a complex amorality to his villains. Here his character thinks no one sees how dangerous he is; he believes he can charm the world. When Walken lets the evil emerge from behind the smile, it's terrifying. Walken plays the scariest guys on earth, and this guy is the scariest of all. Maybe because he's the ultimate, impossible-to-please daddy figure, a daddy who confuses himself with the God of the Old Testament: a daddy of stern retribution and then some.

Nicholas Kazan, director of *Dream Lover*, wrote the screenplay. Modern noir specialist James (*After Dark, My Sweet*) Foley directs. Foley's understanding of the characters and their context makes him a Scorsese of the heartland. Foley captures those endless rural nights with nothing to do and the empty, unemployed days spent waiting for the nights. He shows the frustrations such a modern pastoral life produces and the violence that can provide the only relief.

The supporting cast—anchored by Tracey Walter as the psychotic Patch—includes Keifer Sutherland, Candy Clark, and Crispin Glover. Mary Stuart Masterson debuts; her performance as a budding farmgirl in love with Penn launched her career. She's never been so lusty, tough, or believable.

Since no picture from this period of Penn's career would be complete without an appearance by Madonna, she sings "Live to Tell" over the closing credits. The refrain from the song, sampled and elongated, serves as the backing sound track. The ballad is the most heartfelt and least contrived of her career.

There's plenty of heartbreaking violence and not one minute of it is gratuitous.

Other recommended rentals directed by James Foley:
After Dark, My Sweet

Badlands

All-American art movie :ATTITUDE
Violent, poetic chase drama :MOOD

DIRECTOR: Terrence Malick (1974—U.S.A.)
CAST: Martin Sheen, Sissy Spacek, Warren Oates, Ramon Bieri
IN ENGLISH; COLOR

Martin Sheen and Sissy Spacek in *Badlands*

Few directors have made two films as deliberately idiosyncratic and as widely praised as the films of Terrence Malick. And nobody—except Malick—ever directed two such films and then purposefully never made another.

The reluctant poet of contemporary American cinema, Malick wrote and directed *Badlands* and *Days of Heaven*. Both are studies of the loneliness of the American frontier experience. A loneliness that Malick captures in wide-screen, deep-focus panoramas of magnificent open country that should represent freedom, but instead inspires only dread.

Malick understands the longing that America's wide-open spaces induces in its citizens. And he recognizes that violence is the traditional American response to longings unfulfilled. In pursuit of these fascinations, Malick applies his artist's sensibilities to stories that have all the earmarks of pulp. This contributes to the uniquely American style of his films: high art on low subjects, told with grave irony.

Malick retells the story (as later retold in the Bruce Springsteen song "Nebraska," which was partially inspired by this film) of Charlie Starkweather, the young man of the 1950s considered to be modern America's prototypical rampaging shooter-of-strangers-for-no-good-reason.

Martin Sheen plays a sullen Midwestern loser, a garbageman trapped in a claustrophobic rural town. His low station in life is a constant, irritating contradiction to his self-dramatic outlook—he collects garbage in his best boots, strives to look like James Dean, and drives a custom cut-down hot rod. Every time he aspires to better himself, the world slaps him down. The final indignation occurs when the daddy of his much younger girlfriend (Sissy Spacek) calls him poor white trash to his face and orders him to never see the girl again. Warren Oates plays the daddy with all the rectitude that a hard-earned decent life inspires.

Sheen damns Oates's rectitude and shoots him dead; the young lovers take off. Pursued by an army of policemen, they build a fortress in the forest, dance to transistor radios, and drive aimlessly down the ramrod-straight roads of the desolate Midwest. On their wanderings, Sheen shoots people.

Malick views this brief moment in history as a meaningful phenomenon, if only for its lack of meaning. To capture it properly, Sissy Spacek serves as the narrator/commentator as she reads from her journal of their adventures (based on the actual journal of Starkweather's teenage love). She writes in a breezy, high-school tone, with the mock profundity of a gossip magazine. The gap between the horrible events she witnesses and her flip recordings thereof illuminate her character—and Sheen's. She feels all she's capable of feeling, which ain't much. Sheen feels deeply, but he kills people. Malick finds in their overly generous estimation of themselves a new America a'bornin'.

Sheen and Spacek give the calmest, most detailed performances of their careers. Spacek was quite young, but she acts with uncanny depth. Malick, a knowing director of actors, tamps down their emotions until all superficial mannerisms disappear.

Malick's absolute refusal to reveal his own position on anything—which gives the film its opaque, ironic tone—isn't a bad thing. *Badlands* thrives on Malick's distance, which makes the film funny and profound as well as violent and memorable. A deeply satisfying and engrossing rental: mayhem, scenery, and humor, if you don't want to pay attention; a true American art film if you do.

Other recommended rentals directed by Terrence Malick:

Days of Heaven

Barry Lyndon

Man's fate :**ATTITUDE**
Stately costume/morality epic :**MOOD**

DIRECTOR: Stanley Kubrick (1975—U.K.)
CAST: Ryan O'Neal, Marisa Berenson, Patrick Magee
IN ENGLISH; COLOR

Ryan O'Neal and Marisa Berenson in Barry Lyndon

Adapted from the Thackeray novel and starring Ryan O'Neal, this is a slow, beautiful, tragic, intelligent costume epic, best suited for being at home with the flu or for a long weekend of truly horrific weather. It should be rented when you want to stay indoors, want to be distracted, and recognize that you have an ample store of patience. That said, it's nowhere near as slow or difficult as, say, the most accessible Bergman film—and there are no subtitles.

Barry Lyndon follows the life of a man who will do anything to move up society's ladder and, given what the bottom rungs of it were like in the eighteenth century, who can blame him? Along the way he learns duplicity, sees all of Europe, much of war, breaks hearts, and has his own broken in return. He also duels, fights for the British army, gallivants about the courts of Europe, and makes a place

for himself in English high society—all in sumptuous visual detail.
Kubrick, famous for his attention to detail and research, turns *Barry Lyndon* into a history lesson as well as a drama. Kubrick's costuming is superb and he remains a genuine scholar of classical music, which he employs in his sound tracks with greater skill than any other filmmaker. As usual, Kubrick's compassion for human folly appears to be nil, and his belief in human folly as the source of humor and pathos, absolute.

Because Kubrick needs a big canvas to contain all his ideas, *Barry Lyndon* is a long film. Boy, is it long. Three full, slow hours, and every minute breathtaking; it's worth renting for the landscapes and costumes alone. It's also a textbook in the dress, manners, morals, mores, warfare, conversational styles, art, dining, lighting, and politics of its time. Kubrick went so far as to codesign and fabricate a camera lens that could shoot in candlelight. Every interior scene is lit only with the light that would have been available in the eighteenth century, be it sunlight through windows, from fireplaces, or from candelabras.

Kubrick, very much a nineteenth-century kind of guy, is well suited to making a film about the eighteenth. Kubrick is no modernist; he seldom refers to his own storytelling processes. Kubrick likes the invisible narrative of the theater, with a well-constructed plot, characters who behave in a consistent manner and thematic/emotional cohesion. This provides the slow pace of the film, but it also adds to the complexity of the characters.

And now the bad news: Ryan O'Neal is in every scene. If you dislike him as a performer before the film begins, your love for him will not increase by the time the closing credits roll. But, even if you loathe his acting, his performance does not ruin the film. It's perfectly adequate—in that O'Neal kind of way.

Other recommended rentals directed by Stanley Kubrick:

2001: A Space Odyssey

A Clockwork Orange

Dr. Strangelove or: How I Learned to Stop Worrying and Love the Bomb

The Killing

Full Metal Jacket

Lolita (see page 91)

Paths of Glory (see page 125)

The Battle of Algiers

Docudrama of guerrilla war :**ATTITUDE**
Political action thriller :**MOOD**

DIRECTOR: Gillo Pontecorvo (1965—France)
CAST: Jean Martin, Yacef Saadi
IN FRENCH AND ALGERIAN WITH ENGLISH SUBTITLES; B/W

The quinessential political thriller— a detailed, dramatic, and shockingly documentary-like re-creation of the 1954 Algerian guerrilla war of liberation against France.

Shooting in the Casbah of Algiers, and using non-actors for many of the Algerian

French "Paras" confront Algerian guerrillas in *The Battle of Algiers*

roles, Pontecorvo delivers a dirty, sweaty, enthralling manual on the construction of an urban guerrilla army. He shoots in tight-cornered locations in high-contrast black-and-white for a documentary look, staging bombings and assassinations, gunfights and riots. These are so realistic it's hard to believe he convinced the (post-revolutionary) Algerian government to allow him to so accurately portray their brutality, but he did. When the film was released, most audiences assumed that Pontecorvo intercut documentary footage into dramatic passages, but he did not.

He presents the French with equal, accurate dispassion; the paratroopers who arrive in Algiers to put down the revolution do not hesitate to torture suspects or blow up buildings full of families. The head colonel of the "paras" emerges as a complex villain. Pontecorvo shows the colonel's ruthlessness and his humanity, his willingness to kill and his surgical approach to killing.

While the Algerians, as revolutionaries, wage a war of passion, the French, as mercenaries, wage war for specific results. Pontecorvo presents an Algerian warrior eager to kill every Frenchman he sees and a Frenchman ready to kill nobody if that would achieve his aims. Pontecorvo regards neither man as morally superior; he contends that each warrior is simply the product of his culture, and is fighting the war his respective culture requires.

The colonel, with his sharp cheekbones and expressionless eyes, becomes the soul of the enemy to the Algerians. His tactics prove more effective than theirs, and capturing the leading hero of the revolution becomes his quest. The cat-and-mouse game between the terrorist and the colonel forms the second half of the picture.

At the time of its release—when anti–Vietnam War emotions made everyone an anticolonialist—Pontecorvo's evenhandedness was an act of artistic courage. No one else dared to suggest that a colonial military man could suffer human emotions or be anything but a debauched sadist. Even so, Pontecorvo is clearly on the side of the Algerians, and he presents their bloody victory as an advancement of mankind.

Pontecorvo makes real the promise of *cinéma de la rue*. He shoots like a documentary cameraman eavesdropping on history. His tight framing packs a wallop; the figures in his frames have nowhere to run. While in the Casbah, Pontecorvo shoots the twisting, turning streets with appropriate claustrophobia; on the wide European boulevards near the ocean he opens his frame to suggest the unlimited options available to the wealthy and controlling French.

It's a revolutionary film in form and content. If you have little interest in colonial issues or history, the violence provides constant thrills. If you prefer politics and expertly re-created culture, then the violence serves as plot punctuation. There no are comparable films being made today, films that combine history with drama and make both so compelling.

Other recommended rentals directed by Gillo Pontecorvo:
Burn!

Beyond the Valley of the Dolls

Large-breasted young women and self-parody :ATTITUDE
Brilliant/moronic skin flick of the late 1960s :MOOD

DIRECTOR: Russ Meyer (1970—U.S.A.)
CAST: Dolly Read, Cynthia Myers, Michael Blodgett
IN ENGLISH; COLOR

Marcia M. Broom, Dolly Read, and Cynthia Myers in *Beyond the Valley of the Dolls*

Russ Meyer, a director adoring of scantily clad, large-breasted young women, as most of us adore the breath of life itself, only once in his career stooped (as he saw it) to irony. He now regards this as a lesser effort, but many film scholars rate *Beyond the Valley of the Dolls* as one of the all-time best. And why not?

Film critic Roger Ebert cowrote the darn thing, which concerns several (remarkably) large-breasted, scantily clad young women who—like their forebears in the dreary *Valley of the Dolls*—venture to Hollywood in search of fame. They wear mascara by the truckload, prance around in bikinis, and say things to one another like: "Can't wait to *strap on* your groovy old man."

Meyer's apparent notion of erotica may generate a struggle between guilty laughter and absolute horror. Or, it may shoot you straight into outrage. His sense of humor and political consciousness aim no higher than *Playboy*'s Party Jokes; his idea of sidesplitting humor is a slo-mo close-up of two breasts jiggling in a bikini. Incredibly, it's Meyer's sense of irony that sustains the arguments of those who anoint him genius.

When the realization strikes that no movie could be this moronic on purpose, the sophisticated viewer will discover a knowing lampoon of the Hollywood party scene and the latter days of hippie excess, as perceived by a fifty-year-old breast-obsessed fat guy in a toupee. In his post-1950s, *True Magazine* way, Meyer nails every "Hollywood ambition" convention—sex as a tool for success, the vagaries of luck, the evils of ambition—and inflates them to the point of absurdity.

His take on the hippie culture, though laughably unhip at the time, now seems not so far off the mark. His appropriation of headbands, peace signs, and "Far out, man!" was buffoonish and irritating then. But Meyer understood that these trappings were not sacred objects packed with hidden meaning, but merely the cultural baggage of the moment, ripe for plunder. That insight alone places him light-years ahead of his more reverent and honored contemporaries.

The scenes of the girls attempting to pretend to play their instruments (and make the appropriate rock 'n' roll facial expressions) are especially poignant, but Russ's former Bunnies and doomed starlets convince as well as, say, Frankie Avalon and Annette Funicello. In short, the changing times finally caught up to Meyer's prescience and showed his apparent stupidity to be postmodern perspicacity of the first order.

For overblown self-parody and dialogue beyond over the top, *Beyond* has no peer. The immortal final scene—which blends sex, violence, and parody in a manner guaranteed to bring cardiac arrest and cries for suppression to the politically correct, and uncontrollable hysterical laughter to everyone else—can be neither described nor forgotten.

Neither soft core (it's shockingly tame; barely an R rating, these days) nor comedy, *Beyond* remains a singular cultural artifact, a showpiece of BadFilm.

Other recommended rentals directed by Russ Meyer:
Beneath the Valley of the Ultra-Vixens
Faster Pussycat! Kill! Kill!

Big Wednesday

Grandiose surfer epic **:ATTITUDE**
Wide-screen serious surfer drama **:MOOD**

DIRECTOR: John Milius (1978—U.S.A.)
CAST: Jan-Michael Vincent, Gary Busey, William Katt
IN ENGLISH; COLOR

Director/screenwriter John Milius, seeking to honor his adolescent obsession with surfing, attempts the Great American Movie. Surfing seems a fit subject for Milius's usual mythic approach, and he goes completely grandiose, throwing in Coming of Age, Dodging the Draft, Leaving Home, First Love, First Sex, End of Adolescent Friendship, Onset of Adulthood, Reclaimed Youth, etc.

William Katt in *Big Wednesday*

Milius's screenplays (*The Wind and the Lion, Dillinger*) often celebrate a special kind of American grand-scale stupidity and *Big Wednesday* is, impossibly, even dumber than that. Sacrificing anything resembling subtext, Milius creates an enduring vision of the surfer-as-samurai and of the surf movie as western. In keeping with his western/samurai esthetic, Milius frames his heroes against a vast, wild land—with the ocean substituting for those wide-open spaces—in which no rules exist but those his heroes invent. If you're accustomed to Frankie Avalon on the beach, or the crude 16-mm approach of *Endless Summer*, the heroic frames seem at first ridiculous, then endearing, and finally the only way to treat the subject matter. Even if you've never *seen* an ocean, Milius convinces you that surfing can be a mythic endeavor. Lots of fun, too.

Jan-Michael Vincent, Gary Busey, and William Katt star as three lifelong buddies bound together by their mutual love, respect, appreciation of, and addiction to, surfing. Vincent seems wild, young, and uncorrupted. Busey is hell-raising unchained, as befits his character, and William Katt is convincing as a straitlaced bore. (And that's the main problem with the third quarter of the film: It's boring. Too much simpleminded character development and not enough wave riding.)

Children of the sixties, this gang of brothers gets into scrapes, meets girls, grows up, deals with Vietnam, gets married, and goes their separate ways. One memorable day (the "Big Wednesday" of the title), they return to the beach of their youth for the most metaphorical, most Surfer Samurai–requiring, most male buddyhood–evoking waves in surfer history—and them waves is some *big* suckers, too. The final fifteen minutes are pure joy, as professional surfer stand-ins shred what appear to be endless sets of thirty-footers. It's an all-American epic. And relentlessly stupid, in the best possible way.

Bigger Than Life

Oedipus meets Ozzie and Harriet :**ATTITUDE**
Vivid, suspenseful family drama :**MOOD**

DIRECTOR: Nicholas Ray (1956—U.S.A.)
CAST: James Mason, Barbara Rush, Walter Matthau
IN ENGLISH; COLOR

This is Nicholas Ray's masterful take on the unease, paranoia, desperation, and denial underlying the happy facade of suburban America. Only a savage, sentimental cynic like Ray would depict with equal conviction the affection, loyalty, and endurance of the very family he simultaneously reviles for its hypocrisy. So subversive is this passionate tale of a family gone awry that the studio insisted on a "happy" ending. Ray provides one so patently false as to make you fear for the life of everyone on-screen.

James Mason stars as an all-American 1950s father—the perfect TV dad of the era and a terrifying figure of paternal authority—driven to murderous megalomania by overdoses of a prescription drug. Mason plays a devoted dad, a man who always puts his family first. In the first quarter of the film, Ray inflates Mason's goodness to absurd levels. It's weird and off-putting, until you realize that Ray exaggerates one aspect of Mason's character only to illuminate the other; Mason's superficial flawlessness mirrors the weakness he represses. When Mason's inner demons arise, his assumed persona of perfection provides little defense.

A medical problem leads Mason to an addiction to cortisone. Cortisone was a relatively new drug, and had been prescribed without an understanding of its side effects. Foremost among them is psychosis; Mason goes slowly batty without the slightest notion that his behavior is changing. His family, baffled by Mason's newly critical, abrasive, and finally dangerous self, never considers that drugs might be an issue. When Mason picks them apart or subjects them to torrents of rage, they blame themselves.

Their soul-searching as they seek the source of Mason's nastiness is particularly touching and almost unbearably real. It also presages to an astounding degree the dialogues, thought processes, and rescue attempts of contemporary families facing a drug-addicted relative.

Mason retains just enough of his superficial personality to function, which makes his inexorably emerging dark side all the more terrifying. His increasing (but still deniable) madness brings out every tension lurking in the web of family life. Mason becomes a dominating ogre to his son, who must secretly plot with his mother in order to save Dad. Thus Ray introduces the ever-lurking Oedipal tensions—tensions Mason mocks when he discovers their efforts to control him.

In the most terrifying sequence, and one that underscores Ray's unmatched gift for finding the visual key to complex emotions, the son sneaks into his father's bedroom and opens the forbidden drawer of his father's dresser. Glancing up into the mirror, he sees the enraged face of the man he loves and fears the most.

After many travails, cortisone is discovered as the culprit and Mason is returned to the bosom of his family, happy and whole. The closing shot of Mason hugging his wife and child, all grinning desperately, is

Ray's horrible joke. Via their manufactured joy, Ray makes it clear that Mason's next freak-out is only a matter of time. . . .

A study in double messages—wherein the surface story tells one tale, the visual treatment quite another—the film is beautifully acted and shot in strident Eastman Color, which Ray uses with rare understanding. To Wim Wenders—and to the French directors/film theorists of the New Wave (Godard, Truffaut, Chabrol, etc.)—Nicholas Ray is a god, and this his testament.

Other recommended rentals directed by Nicholas Ray:

In a Lonely Place (see page 71)

Johnny Guitar

Rebel Without a Cause

Black Narcissus

Rent this first! **:ATTITUDE**
Heartbreaking Technicolor drama **:MOOD**

DIRECTORS: Michael Powell, Emeric Pressburger (1946—U.K.)
CAST: Deborah Kerr, David Farrar, Kathleen Byron, Sabu
IN ENGLISH; TECHNICOLOR

One of the all-time greats; a film that every film buff should see at least twice; a psychological drama with a romantic subplot; a study in the symbolic power of color, shadow, light, and form. *Black Narcissus* communicates a different but equally powerful message to children, to adults, to

Deborah Kerr and David Farrar in *Black Narcissus*

men, and to women. If this book induces you to rent only one film you never heard of, let it be *Black Narcissus*.

Director Michael Powell and screenwriter Emeric Pressburger (*The Red Shoes*) worked under the production name The Archers. Their distinctive combination of literate, European perversity and lyrical flowing narrative places them in no tradition but their own. Structuralists par excellence, the Archers' pictures feature a traditional, elegant construction. In a career of willfully intelligent, deliberately subtle, psychologically complex, and finely crafted pictures, this is their most profound, most multileveled work. It's also one of the most beautiful movies ever made, and won Oscars for Best Cinematography and for Production Design. For cinematic poetry, emotion, sets, use of color, classic acting, and dramatic impact, it can't be beat.

Deborah Kerr leads a group of nuns to an abandoned palace high in the Indian Himalayas, intending to create a hospital and school for the local villagers. Once there, they find the atmosphere strangely dislocating. The local people reject civilization with a shrug of their shoulders; their joy in a sensual, pagan life further disarms the nuns. Kerr finds herself recalling, with intrusive passion, life and love in the Scottish village of her birth. Other nuns shirk their duties, or find themselves cast into reverie at the sight of an Indian prince's silk tunic. They experience difficulty tending to their responsibilities after a lifetime of little else. Kerr in particular is frightened to find herself so easily distracted.

Appearing like a genie, as the very incarnation of their forbidden erotic (though not always sexual) longing is David Farrar, who plays the local English colonial authority. Farrar, a leading man of the relaxed, deep-voiced school, finds himself falling for Kerr and she, though she cannot admit it, for him. Farrar plays a man accustomed to following his instincts, and Kerr frustrates him terribly. Another nun, Sister Ruth, more sensitive to her own longings and oppressed by the repression surrounding her, goes mad. As Sister Ruth—played by the ravishing Kathleen Byron—loses her connection with the world of religion she becomes increasingly menacing, beautiful, and sexual.

The Archers create a tragic consideration of the erotic power of memory, of the perverse nature of love, and, depending on your perspective, of either the horror of a life wasted in worship or the noble sacrifices required therefore. They present an implicit debate on the relative merits of civilization versus primitivism, of acting-out versus repression, and of reason versus emotion.

The Archers consider these issues with the gravity they warrant, and yet produce a coherent, commercial drama driven by a compelling love story. They raise no question, however serious, without a light touch and dashing wit.

The story operates powerfully on both the conscious level—a tale of nuns dealing with a loss of faith and direction—and on the unconscious—the battle against memory, the lure of self-destruction, and the oppressive safety of duty. The Archers use color and shadow to represent emotion; their ability to place characters in a frame to illustrate one character's relationship to another is unmatched; they shift from past to present as if in a dream and call upon a veritable storehouse of Jungian, Freudian, symbolist, and poetic imagery.

A complex work of art and an enduring piece of entertainment.

Other recommended rentals directed by Michael Powell and/or Emeric Pressburger:

49th Parallel (see page 51)
I Know Where I'm Going (see page 68)
The Life and Times of Colonel Blimp
Peeping Tom (see page 127)
The Red Shoes
The Small Back Room
Thief of Bagdad (1940; see page 172)

Bob le Flambeur

Minimalist cool :**ATTITUDE**
Ironic French gangsters :**MOOD**

DIRECTOR: Jean-Pierre Melville (1955—France)
CAST: Robert Duchesne, Isabel Corey, Guy Decomble
IN FRENCH WITH ENGLISH SUBTITLES; B/W

Writer/director/auteur Jean-Pierre Melville made deceptively simple noirs. His direct storytelling, cynical wit, handheld camera, and use of street patois made him the forerunner of the French film movement known as *cinéma de la rue*. His hard-boiled dialogue and crisp visual language made him a mentor to a generation of young American film directors (Scorsese and Coppola among them), who sought out his work when no one in this country remembered it. Melville's influence was equally powerful among the young turks of the French New Wave: Truffaut, Godard, and Rivette, anyone who sought to shoot on the streets rather than in a studio, and who found in handheld black-and-white the poetry of subversion. Melville wrote dialogue to match his visuals: spare, clipped, and functional.

Bob le Flambeur's opening shot—a slow, jerky pan of Montmartre at night—established Melville as a low-budget master. Melville's understated cinema delivers the following message: "I have no money. I know nothing of technique. I'm not a fancy guy. But, I know my characters, I know my atmosphere, and I will not lie or manipulate. Here is my story, told with truth, please enjoy. And, remember, these gangsters are also mythic creatures who carry the good and evil in all of us. Look closely and you may recognize yourself."

Bob le Flambeur (Bob the Gambler) is one of cinema's enduring constructions, a completely modern (for the 1950s) heroic model for an entirely French sensibility. Cooler than James Bond, always relaxed and in charge, Bob drives a big American convertible slowly, slowly through the rain-slick, late-night streets of Paris, holding the wheel casually with one hand while the other dangles stylishly out the window.

Bob is never without his buckled overcoat or his oversized fedora (on him it looks good); he both protects and falls for wayward angels of the Montmartre night. Cool as he is, Bob cannot resist the ennui of encroaching middle age. He gets a crackpot idea for one last big heist. Bob plans and schemes with all his coolness intact, but you know about pesky old fate . . . and no one is more fatalistic than Melville.

While most noir of the period villainized women for their sexual hunger, Melville practically worships one of the most amoral femme fatales in movie history. The magnificent, sixteen-year-old Isabel Corey jumps in and out of beds, satiating herself and breaking hearts without a backward glance. Melville not only does not condemn, he congratulates Isabelle on her ability to rule her admittedly tiny world with no more powerful a weapon than her own carnality. Her casual, erotic nudity is a shocking surprise when *Bob* is compared to American films of the same era.

As Melville himself stated, *Bob* is not quite a noir; it's more a comedy of manners, in which the cops and crooks adhere to a rigorous, though never spoken, code of conduct. Melville is interested in atmosphere rather than crime, in young lust and old folly, in style and its power.

The result is charming, light and enjoyable. The story zips along agreeably, and it may only be afterward that you realize how skillfully Melville has created this imaginary, romantic world that for the previous ninety minutes seemed so real. A simple masterpiece, a triumph of wit and style.

Other recommended rentals directed by Jean-Pierre Melville:
Le Samourai

A Boy and His Dog

Adolescent sci-fi :**ATTITUDE**
Low-budget postapocalyptic adventure :**MOOD**

DIRECTOR: L.Q. Jones (1975—U.S.A.)
CAST: Don Johnson, Jason Robards, Susanne Benton, Tim McIntire
IN ENGLISH; COLOR

A straightforward, funny, and nasty futurist tale made in the manner of American International Pictures exploitation flicks: low budget, high talent, and constant, deliberate self-referential wit. This winning combo means solid kicks for the younger target audience, amusement for the knowing postadolescent.

Don Johnson—and a real baby he was, too, so young as to be unrecognizable except for his self-satisfied leer—roams the desert wastelands of a post–nuclear holocaust America. He has three goals: to eat, to survive, and to get laid. In pursuit of those goals he robs, kills, and dreams—there are no women to be found. Numerous feral gangs, in gear and attitude that prefigure *The Road Warrior,* also roam the desert, looking to murder (or even eat) the weak and to enslave the strong. Moving stealthily through a cleverly sparse (bear in mind the budget restrictions) chaos, Johnson struggles to stay free. His ally in this struggle? His dog, who speaks to him telepathically in the wry, bemused voice of the outstanding, underrated late character actor, Tim McIntire.

Johnson drifts from encampment to encampment, playing crazy tricks that evoke a paternal but admiring response from the dog. While the boy and the dog need and love one another, they recognize, to their mutual frustration, that the dog is smarter than the boy. He uses words the boy doesn't understand; he quotes authors of whom the boy has never heard; he advises caution as the boy leaps into the void. They make a perfect pair: the dog thinks, the boy acts. The boy listens carefully to the dog's advice in all matters excepting those pertaining to libido.

The dog sniffs out a girl. Despite the dog's warnings, Johnson follows the girl to as eloquent an image as any postapocalyptic exploitation film ever offered: a single door standing in the middle of the desert. She lures him in and he's kidnapped into an underground world of plenty: food, luxury, and women. The underground survivors—led by Jason Robards in one of his inexplicable, self-amused trash-movie turns—need the boy's sperm. They've been underground so long they're all infertile: Please insert the low-budget sci-fi explanation of your choice here.

Johnson is pleased by the notion of impregnating a nation, but horrified by the totalitarian, underground world of robotic cheerleaders and Stepfordian housewives. The filmmaker's quaint notions of social satire, conceived as a slap at the Nixonian universe, now appear romantic indeed, as all of the director's worst nightmares of externally enforced social values seem to have come true. Johnson, a true adolescent, much prefers the fatal anarchy of life above to the safe conformity of life below. He escapes with the girl and reunites with his dog, who lies starving in wait on the surface. The girl, the boy, and the dog face one final ethical/philosophical dilemma. . . .

Everyone seemed to have had a good time making this likable adventure. The first half, with its chases, fights, and creation of a desolate world, offers more punch and punch lines than Johnson's journey beneath the surface. Director Jones renders the oppressive, noisy underground a bit too oppressively, and when the dog's offscreen, Johnson's just not as interesting.

A clever, entertaining effort in a consistently rewarding, everdwindling, and much-missed American genre: smart, cheap trash.

Cabeza de Vaca

Surreal conquistadors :**ATTITUDE**
Nightmarish arty travelogue/adventure :**MOOD**

DIRECTOR: Nicolas Echevarria (1993—Spain)
CAST: Juan Diego, Daniel Ormenez Cacho, Roberto Sosa, Carlos Castañon
IN SPANISH WITH ENGLISH SUBTITLES; COLOR

A journey into avant-garde, nonnarrative filmmaking, and mystical, mythical legend based on historical fact. Reminiscent of the loopy metaphor-fest *El Topo* in its mad intensity and prevalence of religious allegory, this tall tale—think Dalí, El Greco, and Buñuel—is far less pretentious, more heartfelt and inspired: a genuine, transcendent religious experience.

Spanish knight Álvar Núñez Cabeza de Vaca was shipwrecked on the coast of Texas in 1527 with three hundred men. He then traveled across the Southwest, a trip that required years. Miraculously, he and his surviving crewmen were rescued by the wandering expedition of Hernando Cortez. Cabeza de Vaca wrote of his adventures, and this film is the adaptation of his manuscript.

The director dispenses with two staples of Hollywood filmmaking: cogent narrative and the linking of any two scenes in continuous time. Time transitions occur abruptly and for no apparent reason. This abrupt shifting from one scene, one locale, one event to another forms the basis of the film's hypnotic and dreamlike aspect.

De Vaca, captured by a Seminole *brujo* and tortured daily, experiences a religious awakening so strong even the *brujo* recognizes it as such. He sets de Vaca free, who wanders, as a messiah must. In his wandering he discovers—and loses at the worst possible moment—the power to raise the dead by the laying-on of hands. (Faith is presented to him, faith is taken away.) With this power he becomes an angel to the violent and indecipherable tribes of the desert Southwest. Without it, he's considered an impostor, a demon to be feared and killed.

As he wanders, Indian attacks occur, often introduced with a hail of arrows that appears with no apparent connection to the previous scene. Tibetan music bangs away in the background for much of the film, which is presented at a pace to allow glaciers to go whizzing by. Shooting in wide screen, the director packs every inch of his frame—both from side to side and deeply, back to front—with strange, mutant desert landscapes, murderous rituals, hallucinatory sunsets, and nauseatingly gory close-ups of violence.

Sound familiar? Well, it should—it's an astounding, multileveled visual equivalent to the prose of Cormac McCarthy, author of *All the Pretty Horses, The Crossing,* and especially *Blood Meridian.* Though in this crazed world, no horses run across the strange, bloody landscape: Cabeza de Vaca and his compatriots lost their horses in the shipwreck and so had to walk. When a ragged band of Cortez's conquistadors appear, the Indians are paralyzed with awe and horror at their first sighting of men on horseback. By shooting the oncoming riders at a distance, the director makes it clear how the Indians might easily mistake the two—horse and man—for a single, unholy beast.

For all the strangeness, infinite spells without a word of dialogue, and explicit violence, there's also plenty of cool western action, plus landscapes out of nightmares, of dreams, of Eden, and of Hell. The director is quite taken with the countryside around him, and he takes a time-out from the plot to share these landscapes whenever he feels like it.

If you're accustomed to slow, arty films, if you know and like the work of Werner Herzog, then rent without reservation. Otherwise, consider whether you can bear the slow pace, the unending savagery, the clanging music, the absence of anything resembling explanation and the (be warned) overwhelmingly powerful emotion. . . . If so, this may prove one of the enduring filmic experiences of your life. If not, you'll be bored to death.

Candy Mountain

Pastoral road movie :**ATTITUDE**
Open country, psychodrama, open country :**MOOD**

DIRECTORS: Robert Frank, Rudy Wurlitzer (1987—Canada)
CAST: Kevin J. O'Connor, Harris Yulin, Bulle Ogier, David Johansen
IN ENGLISH; COLOR

Whether American road movies extract "speed kills" kicks or sweet melancholy from the wide-open spaces, their usual message is that the road offers redemption, knowledge, useful hard knocks, and, almost always, a cataclysm at the end—the cataclysm being the inevitable dues that must be paid for the freedom the road provides.

The 1950s Beats celebrated the road as the place where an American found himself (they didn't write too much about women) by his contrasts and/or similarities with "Real America," which could be discovered only On the Road. And by the contemplative opportunities offered by sitting in a car day after day, watching the real America glide by. Coming well after the Beats, but understanding plenty about freedom and dues, *Candy Mountain* delivers a more complex take on the road and on the road movie.

A bumbling youth—played by Kevin J. O'Connor, as the essence of a rebel without a clue—dreams of being a rock 'n' roller. He meets a couple of big-timers living out the rock-star lifestyle he craves: David Johansen and Joe Strummer. Their determination and strangeness should convince him that he's too lame to live their life, but he's too lame to understand. The rock honchos give Kevin a mysterious assignment: to track down the elusive Elmore Silk (Harris Yulin), maker of the world's greatest custom guitars.

Kevin argues with his girlfriend, who dumps him at a highway rest stop. The car is hers, he has to hitchhike and his journey is launched. The wandering asphalt path takes him from one adventure to another: He's locked in a cage by a perverted constable, unknowingly assists in a break-in, has a wild night of passion with French film goddess Bulle Ogier, and flees the all-too-eager arms of a frontier woman so desperate for company she might never let him leave.

Kevin tracks down Elmore Silk, and discovers a man who has seen rock 'n' roll from top to bottom and despises it; he hates his own guitars even more. O'Connor's half-baked notions of rebel integrity receive a jolt when he observes Silk's eagerness to sell himself to the highest bidder. Silk should be the sage at the end of the quest, the all-knowing guru to straighten O'Connor out, but Kevin doesn't heed the message.

He finds himself back on the road, heading home, broke, confused, and not that much wiser. There's no cataclysm, no blinding flash of revelation; Kevin has learned only the first lesson of the road: The road goes on forever.

The directorial team includes the great still photographer Robert Frank, and one of the wackier screenwriters, Rudy Wurlitzer (*Pat Garrett & Billy the Kid* (see page 123). Frank composes in rich, sensual colors and deliberately casual frames; he shoots mostly in wide angle so we never lose the power of the landscape. Wurlitzer proves to be a gifted director of actors; the performances are low key and the dialogue conversational. The casting couldn't be more self-consciously hip, but it works: Tom Waits, Leon Redbone, Dr. John, and even Laurie Metcalf appear, and all do a creditable job.

Though the camera work is simple (due to a low budget), there are images of heartbreaking poetry. Frank's visuals support a core value of road movies: There's profundity in the open landscape of the outback and only the road can take you there.

The Chase

Edgy potboiler **:ATTITUDE**
Melodrama with stars **:MOOD**

DIRECTOR: Arthur Penn (1965—U.S.A.)
CAST: Marlon Brando, Angie Dickinson, Jane Fonda, Robert Redford,
     E.G. Marshall
IN ENGLISH; COLOR

What a pedigree for a basic melodrama of one wild night in an overheated Texas town! The screenplay, by playwright Lillian Hellman, is based on the play by Horton Foote (*Tender Mercies*). Arthur Penn (*The Missouri Breaks*—see page 107) directs a cast thick with stars: Marlon Brando, Robert Redford in his screen debut, Jane Fonda, E.G. Marshall, Angie Dickinson, Robert Duvall, James Fox, and Janice Rule.

Robert Redford and Jane Fonda in *The Chase*

The men swagger around in tight suits and cowboy boots, and the women shimmy in those clingy 1965 cocktail dresses that show lots of cleavage. Everyone's doing it with everyone else's wife, or wants to, only the men are passionless drunks and the women frigid neurotics (1960s psychobabble alert!), so nobody does anything except talk. On a night when everyone in town is partying, Bubba (Robert Redford) escapes from prison.

Everybody knows that Bubba will head straight home to reclaim his wife, played by a young Jane Fonda. Jane's uptight lover—James Fox—insists that the sheriff (played by Marlon Brando) *do* something. Marlon tries, but the town power structure insists on interfering. The rapidly escalating disorder releases the town's repressed energies, for good or ill.

Everyone's corrupt little secrets get exposed and the town ignites (literally) in an orgy of race and class hatred and good old-fashioned Texas savagery. A lynch mob beats the crap out of the sheriff, several marriages break up, and half the town burns to the ground.

The story drifts occasionally into soap opera, but the cast seems to recognize its moment in the sun. Some ham it up unforgivably; some knock your socks off, Duvall and Fonda among them. Redford's nascent charisma is intriguing, but he's no match for Brando. Marlon dominates the ensemble with an unusually controlled performance. He plays the (unwanted) conscience of the town, the man whose thankless job is to serve the law and everyone's petty interests simultaneously. He fails at both tasks.

From a dull opening—a slow grinding through the gears of scene-setting and establishing the tortuously involved back-story—Penn develops impressive momentum. He builds from the harmless fun of the drunken upper classes to the homicidal intent of the lower, whose violence is depicted as a traditional acting-out of the repressed wishes of their masters. Hellman's screenplay captures all the creepiness of the age-old interaction between the small-town redneck and his patron. This was a particularly resonant insight into the American South at the time of the filming, and served as Penn's allegorical protest against the racial violence occurring.

A dark, pessimistic, big-budget drama featuring several unpredictable turns, crazy dialogue, superb (and ghastly) performances, the first inclination of Penn's gift for cinematic mayhem, and numerous high-minded messages. A bit slow, a bit obvious; a film you can thoroughly enjoy even as you make wisecracks back at the screen.

Other recommended rentals directed by Arthur Penn:
Bonnie and Clyde
The Missouri Breaks (see page 107)
Night Moves

The Conformist

Art movie :**ATTITUDE**
Beautiful, cinematic tale of intrigue :**MOOD**

DIRECTOR: Bernardo Bertolucci (1969—Italy)
CAST: Jean-Louis Trintignant, Dominique Sanda, Pierre Clementi
IN ITALIAN WITH ENGLISH SUBTITLES; COLOR

Only once did Bertolucci combine his poet's observations of the bottomless trickery of the heart with his fascination for cinema itself. Happily, he was young enough to enjoy playing around with plot structure and innocent enough (by Bertoluccian standards) to feel compassion for his characters.

At the height of his powers, and free of the self-conscious, over-analysis that slows much of his later work, Bertolucci presents his favorite themes: alienation, sexual confusion, Oedipal rage, incredible risks taken to slake momentary lust, self-delusion, really nice clothes, exquisite interiors, styles of the 1930s, the looming architecture of Paris, the allure/danger of women, and the anguishes and gratifications of betrayal.

An anonymous man (Bertolucci's favorite kind), desperate to squelch his inner confusion, joins the Fascist Party in prewar Italy, seeking in mass identity a perfection to replace his own tragically flawed individuality. This cultured, repressed Everyman marries a passionate but idiotic woman in an attempt to become normal, to conform. Anxious to escape his father's madness and his mother's infidelity, the Conformist yearns to serve as a model Fascist. At the Party's behest, he takes on the assignment of assassinating his former professor and suffers ambivalence when he falls in love with the professor's wife. She might or might not love the Conformist, but she certainly desires his wife.

Intrigues follow, and the plot, for all its time-shifting, is fairly conventional, though difficult to follow on first viewing. Bertolucci jumps around constantly, flashbacking through the Conformist's life. The flashbacks follow his tormented thinking and reveal his complex character with remarkable clarity. It helps to remember that "the present" is the Conformist riding in a car driven by his

Fascist assistant, en route to kill the professor. All flashbacks return to that ride, until they catch up to the present and events proceed.

Reveling in costumes, cinematography, and set design, Bertolucci attempts nothing less than a visual history of the cinema, employing every style from the earliest days of silent film onward, so that as the plot advances, the cinematic styles grow increasingly modern. From a static camera to tracking shots to handheld chase scenes, Bertolucci demonstrates his singular gift, matching every shot to the emotional content of each scene.

As he uses landscape in *The Sheltering Sky* (see page 153), so Bertolucci uses architecture here as a source of information about the characters, as frame-defining monuments, and as a scale against which his characters measure themselves. When the Conformist visits the Fascist headquarters, he's lost in the marble immensity of the hall; his father's lunatic asylum is a surreal outdoor theater in which his father plays a doomed Lear.

Bertolucci's sense of the cultural, sexual, and psychological mood of the early days of Italian Fascism seems preternaturally subtle and acute. Bertolucci also understands thoroughly the soul of each of his characters—of how many directors can that be said?

Other recommended rentals directed by Bernardo Bertolucci:
The Last Emperor
Last Tango in Paris
The Sheltering Sky (see page 153)

Contempt

Godard and Bardot :**ATTITUDE**
Profound, ironic art movie :**MOOD**

DIRECTOR: Jean-Luc Godard (1963—France/Italy)
CAST: Michel Piccoli, Brigitte Bardot, Jack Palance, Fritz Lang
IN FRENCH WITH ENGLISH SUBTITLES; COLOR

Godard's gift is the gift of cinema itself: the ineffable combination of photographic composition, acting, and editing that no other art form approximates. Godard understands cinema perhaps too well; his insights into how camera movement and even light itself can evoke emotion led him to abandon narrative early in his career. Maybe he found straight-up storytelling dull and obvious, maybe he found better uses for the sacred frame than melodramas of good versus evil. Godard's insight may be too multileveled and abstract for the whole storytelling *thing*, which he saw as bourgeois and confining.

Brigitte Bardot in *Contempt*

Visually, this is his most accessible tale, his most straightforward storytelling. Adapted from the novel, *Le Mepris*, it follows a screenwriter (Michel Piccoli) who must decide whether to write a commercial corruption of Homer's *Odyssey* for a crass American film producer, played with brash, iconic enthusiasm by Jack Palance. None other than Brigitte Bardot plays Piccoli's wife.

As the film begins, Piccoli and Bardot are deeply in love. Piccoli's moral quandary—whether to write commercial garbage—leads him into paralyzing indecision and a strange willingness to kowtow to the monied, authoritarian Palance. When Bardot suspects—incorrectly—that Piccoli might trade her to Palance for success, she develops a growing contempt for him. When Piccoli begs to know what he has done, Bardot cannot or does not say.

While Godard loves to tell of love going wrong, he loves movies more. Incorporating the filming of a film into his film gives Godard the opportunity to race through more dazzling cinematic jokes than a lecture hall of film scholars could cipher: The legendary director Fritz Lang plays the on-screen director of the *Odyssey* picture; Godard's camera shoots into other cameras; Palance delivers hilarious producer-type speeches; sinuous tracking shots snake the length of Bardot's body; Bardot lies naked on a Capri rooftop with only an open book—*The Films of Fritz Lang*—covering her behind. . . . These jokes serve the greater tragedy of the love story and are rendered with much affection.

These passages, and those of Piccoli in torment over the loss of Bardot, are among the most sincere in Godard's oeuvre. Piccoli is baffled; he honestly cannot tell whether he's relinquishing his integrity, and so opts for passivity. Godard makes it clear that to sacrifice artistic freedom means surrendering the right to be worthy of love.

Mainstream movies have incorporated so many of the techniques Godard invented that *Contempt* is neither dated nor difficult to understand. No one ever used color like Godard. Splashes of yellow or especially red (Godard: "I don't show blood, I show the color red.") blast onto the screen to underscore the character's emotions. Godard's camera movement, coupled with Georges Delarue's haunting score, evokes wrenching emotions; this is a tragedy (lost love) played out inside a farce (Piccoli's endless blather over self-prostitution). Such complexities should require explanation: How can Godard create so much heartache simply by moving the camera?

Other recommended rentals directed by Jean-Luc Godard:

Alphaville
Breathless
Masculin/Feminin
Pierrot le Fou
Tout Va Bien
Weekend

Cutter's Way (aka Cutter and Bone)

Justifiable paranoia :**ATTITUDE**
Downbeat character-driven mystery/suspense :**MOOD**

DIRECTOR: Ivan Passer (1981—U.S.A.)
CAST: John Heard, Jeff Bridges, Lisa Eichhorn
IN ENGLISH; COLOR

The releasing studio, displeased with the minuscule first-week grosses, changed the title from *Cutter and Bone,* which they considered too depressing, to *Cutter's Way,* which sounds *so* much more lighthearted. Either way, no one went to see this dark thriller, and it vanished in a week, to be remembered as a benchmark of both subdued filmmaking and inept marketing.

Neither precisely noir nor a "Dreiserian study of American disaffection," this willfully ambivalent suspense thriller follows Cutter—an alcoholic, provocative, and terribly disfigured Vietnam vet—in his obsessive pursuit of a rich local landowner, whom Cutter believes committed a murder. Bone, a going-nowhere, yacht-club party boy, is Cutter's best friend. He joins the hunt to amuse himself but becomes as fixated as (the possibly insane) Cutter. Cutter's neglected wife stays home and drinks. Cutter drinks with her, with Bone, and with anyone who will buy him a round. Cutter's wife and Bone may be in love; Cutter may be encouraging them to have an affair. Nobody is certain about anything, except Cutter: He's certainly pissed off.

Cutter's crippled body gives him good reason to so adore despair, but his wife and Bone *choose* anomie; they've given up. Cutter's quest consumes him because he hopes (a) to force someone to kill him since he lacks the courage to kill himself, and (b) to infuse in his wife and in Bone the desire, however remote or ill-founded, to persevere.

Jeff Bridges plays Bone, John Heard is Cutter, and the seldom-seen Lisa Eichhorn plays Cutter's wife. Their performances are astonishing: low-key, neorealist, and in perfect sync with the quiet, foreboding rhythm of the screenplay. Everything in the film, from love to friendship to clues about the murder, is soaked in ambiguity. Credit the many simultaneous moods of the screenplay, which manages to be spellbinding, funny, bitter, hopeful, and tragic without ever becoming self-important or manipulative.

Director Ivan Passer shoots in dark, somber tones. He begins the mystery in darkest night and lashing rain; he ends it in that pitiless California sunshine that so encourages the blessed and so embarrasses the downtrodden. The savage story is redeemed by the brutal honesty of its depiction, the razor-sharp dialogue, and Passer's documentary-like evocation of the lives of California's working poor and idle rich.

Passer trusts that his characters and a simple narrative style will reveal the profundity of his themes. He doesn't beat you over the head with the depth of his perception, and his picture loses none of its entertainment value for being such a downer. However memorable the characters, the murder mystery drives the plot and its suspense never slackens.

Deep Cover

Smart action **:ATTITUDE**
Edgy, articulate cop thriller **:MOOD**

DIRECTOR: Bill Duke (1992—U.S.A.)
CAST: Laurence Fishburne, Jeff Goldblum, Clarence Williams III
IN ENGLISH; COLOR

Laurence Fishburne, Clarence Williams III, and Jeff Goldblum in *Deep Cover*

It's a classic B-movie cop thriller with a twist, set in the L.A. cocaine trade. The twist?—the cop and the crook are the same guy: Larry Fishburne, starring as the smoothest man in America. The second-smoothest is Jeff Goldblum, all corruption and ambition, who becomes Fishburne's best friend and, simultaneously, the twisted mirror image of his conscience. Fishburne is the essence of reticence and hipster restrained reaction. Goldblum is the overanxious middle-class kid grown up, desperate to convince the world he isn't as scared as everybody knows he is. Both serve as the other's fatal flaw: Who will crack first?

Fishburne plays an undercover cop recruited to pose as a dope dealer and ordered to infiltrate the world of big-time cocaine trafficking. He proves far too skilled at his new assignment, and unforeseen moral and career choices threaten to overwhelm him. As Fishburne sinks into a stylish mire of violence and money, he partners up with Goldblum, who plays a lawyer with utopian dreams of dope-fulfilled riches and no shortage of trenchant insights. It's weird to see Goldblum shoot people, but with his beady eyes and newly hulking build, he makes a convincing if unlikely action-toy.

Fishburne gets so deep into his new life he forgets on which side of the legal fence he belongs. There to remind him is Clarence Williams III—Linc from *The Mod Squad*—playing the king of square-John policemen. Williams's subtle cameo is only one example of the charming hipness running throughout. Director Bill Duke is a black actor best known for action roles in *Predator* (see page 134) and the like. He directs with seriousness and wit, producing stellar performances, great B-movie lighting, and inspired, old-fashioned scene transitions. His sense of pace is perfect; the story never lags.

The script—by Michael Tolkin, author of *The Player* and director of *The New Age*—features Tolkin's highly developed sense of irony. While Tolkin's knowing approach generates most of the lasting pleasure, it never interferes with the more immediately gratifying, traditional elements of classic cop action: shoot-outs, car chases, sex scenes, streetwise slang, and explicit violence. Tolkin's insistence that all his characters show both idiosyncrasy and intelligence makes this an action flick of unusual, if not literary, depth. Tolkin also creates the least stereotypical, most fully formed black characters in any film of recent memory.

Enveloping the story, but never detracting from it or becoming propaganda, is a dead-on summation of the big-time politics of the coke trade and the class war inherent therein.

Cynical? Oh my, yes. Swell shoot-outs. Hilarious one-liners. Smart fun.

Delicatessen

Live-action cartoon :ATTITUDE
Lovable surreal comedy/love story :MOOD

DIRECTORS: Jean-Marie Jeunet, Marc Caro (1991—France)
CAST: Dominique Pinon, Marie-Laure Dougnac, Jean-Claude
   Dreyfus
IN FRENCH WITH ENGLISH SUBTITLES; COLOR

A genuine curiosity, an art comedy of singular visual style: a lyric tale of love and cannibalism told in the lurid colors and lunatic-asylum framing of a comic book. Despite a narrative theme of human flesh sold by the pound, at the film's core resides a gentle fable of innocent love triumphant. And, it's very, very funny.

A kindly circus performer straggles out of a city ravaged by war to the supposed safety of a remote boardinghouse. Little does he know that the inhabitants have been dining on passing strangers since the famine began. The boardinghouse owner—an under-employed butcher by trade—offers the new lodger a job only to fatten him up for his inevitable slaughter. But the owner's daughter falls for the sweet little guy, thus postponing his being carved into stew.

The lady upstairs keeps attempting suicide, the femme fatale makes love to the butcher in exchange for meat, and the bullying postman pursues the butcher's daughter and gleefully awaits the demise of the circus performer. The lodgers draw lots to see who's next, while the mysterious troglodytes continue their subversive campaign from underground.

Everyone comes together in a gravity-defying finale that mixes *It's a Mad, Mad, Mad, Mad World* with thirty years of French New Wave cinema and twenty years of underground comics. The weird-angle action shots and insane stunts suggest Spielberg on LSD: a childlike and good-hearted imagination run completely riot.

Framed like a dream and lit like a distant memory, this fairy tale springs from the fevered brows of two Frenchmen of apparently un-limited visual imagination. Their style—which appears perfectly honed in this, their first feature—combines circus acts, the visual anarchy of comics, deadpan physical comedy à la Buster Keaton, and a surrealist's affection for the grotesque. They prefer actors with exaggerated features, folks sprung full-blown from a sideshow. They shoot these human animations in superclose wide-angle frames, the better to distort their already bulging eyeballs, monumental noses, mountainous bellies, and rocketlike breasts.

The film's cultured slapstick falls into two categories: (1) traditional clowning: pratfalls, unexpected movement, funny faces, and funny sex; or (2) detailed, complex camera moves minutely choreographed to the tiniest motions performed by the actors.

It's baroque, it's ornate, it appears impossible, it's never dull, and underlying the more or less nonstop chaos is a most palpable air of sweet sadness. There's none of the emotional ruthlessness or condescension toward a character's pain that so marks modern American comedies. These guys have sympathy even for the worst of cannibals. For their gentle protagonist, who dances with a monkey, plays a musical saw, and bumbles his way to true love, the filmmakers have only the greatest respect.

A fine date movie, and a good movie for older kids. Best appreciated by film fanatics or those accustomed to the pace of European art films, but not at all difficult or inaccessible.

Other recommended rentals directed by Jean-Marie Jeunet and Marc Caro:

The City of Lost Children

The Dogs of War

Unapologetic war movie **:ATTITUDE**
Straightforward, noisy action-fest **:MOOD**

DIRECTOR: John Irvin (1980—U.K.)
CAST: Christopher Walken, Tom Berenger, Jobeth Williams
IN ENGLISH, SOME FRENCH; COLOR

Paul Freeman, Christopher Walken, Tom Berenger, and Jean F. Stevenin in *The Dogs of War*

An intelligent, hard-boiled, unapologetic war movie—based on an unapologetic best-seller—featuring plenty of well-executed gratuitous violence and little interest in smoothing over the moral ambiguities, which makes the action seem more adult, more real-world. Coolest/creepiest guy in the world, Christopher Walken, plays an almost burnt-out mercenary hired to overthrow an African dictatorship. Suspense is added when his supposedly good-guy employers turn out to be fronting for a large (and evil) commercial concern.

Director John Irvin, working from Frederick Forsythe's pro-colonialist, almost racist (certainly *not* p.c.) novel of mercenaries in Africa, opts for a simple visual language that's just sufficiently bigger than TV to remind us we're at the movies. Irvin explains nothing, sacrificing almost all background and/or character development. Irvin's method demands attention; it also makes for taut action sequences, without a single wasted frame. Such an approach, by definition, excludes sentimentality.

Irvin's reductivism offers a violent world populated by violent guys; neither he nor they have time for social niceties. So, nothing slows down the story. Peripheral characters come and go like trains in the night, and they're on-screen for precisely the right amount of time. Likewise, Irvin's refusal to use subtitles when French, German, or various African tongues are spoken only adds to the ruthless momentum. Every character save Walken's is a sketch, but the sketches are filled in nicely. Walken as a character explains even less than the film; he moves at an equivalent breakneck pace. The boy's got *serious* demons: He seems trapped inside his own body; he hates to kill but lives for it nonetheless. Nothing new there, right? At least as far as conflicted war-guys go. But, don't forget, this is Christopher Walken.

Given Walken's current stature as the absolute icon of Alternative Cool, it's weird to see him play a "John Wayne" action hero, but he does a creditable job. He's more believable away from the killing fields, where he dares not open up and feel what he really feels: nothing. Day-to-day routine is fatal for Chris, battle is the staff of life. He and his band of mercenary cohorts seek not only the thrill of action (which makes the drudgery of ordinary life bearable), but also to emerge victorious on the side of the righteous.

That complex quest climaxes in one really swell, big-scale, nonstop war-movie action set piece, as you know it must. It's a breakneck, elongated orgasm after just the right amount of foreplay.

A film for those who, when young, built model cars so they could pour glue on them, stick firecrackers in them, and set them on fire.

In other words, (guilty) fun for boys.

Don't Look Back

The first rockumentary :**ATTITUDE**
Intimate backstage portrait from another era :**MOOD**

DIRECTOR: D.A. Pennebaker (1965—U.S.A.)
CAST: Bob Dylan, Bobby Neuwirth, Joan Baez, Donovan
IN ENGLISH; B/W

What an annoying little runt this Bob Dylan guy was.

Compelling, though, as proven by this documentary of his 1964 tour of England. Dylan used that tour to jettison the folkie scene that had nurtured him and to launch himself into the (more combative) rocker identity that would shelter him throughout his career.

The film opens with Dylan standing on a New York City corner, staring nastily into the lens. He flips lyric cards for "Subterranean

Homesick Blues" as the (then-indecipherable) song blasts on the sound track. The song ends, Dylan sneers, tosses the cards into the gutter, and Allen Ginsberg strolls across the street, smiling.

The intro sets the tone. Dylan shares events with the camera, but events do not define him; he remains elusive, opaque. For those who know Dylan only as a guy who opened for the Grateful Dead, this may serve as the Original Text. In 1964 Dylan was rebellious pop culture incarnate, and its first rock star. Not a pop star, who looked good and sang catchy tunes (à la Beatles), but a harbinger of rock stars to come, whose stardom was based on the integrity of their eccentric vision. No wonder Dylan worked so hard at being unknowable.

Director—and cinema verité pioneer—D.A. Pennebaker shoots in long, comprehensive takes. Because Pennebaker had only one camera, he pans back and forth constantly to capture both participants in a conversation. Otherwise Pennebaker employs a wide-angle lens, enabling us to witness intimate conversations as well as the room that surrounds them. This adds to the sense of intimacy, of witnessing a secret life made public.

Pennebaker got backstage access no director or cameraman has enjoyed before or since, so we experience numerous archetypal rock-scene scenes. Dylan, apparently smoking pot in a jam-packed hotel room, freaks out when someone pitches a bottle through the window to the street below, thereby bringing the cops. Dylan's agent and an English booker connive to squeeze the BBC out of a few bucks in a seldom-seen apotheosis of backroom sleaze; Brit folkie Donovan sings for Bob, and the entire room holds its breath, awaiting Bob's verdict. "Good song," he says; everybody nods.

Dylan's the sun around which the world revolves and there's no shortage of historical figures desperate to shine in his light. Joan Baez clings to him, Donovan practically genuflects, and Alan Price of the Animals shamelessly kisses ass. In between historical acoustic live performances, Dylan pitilessly shreds anyone—British reporters, a British evangelist, Alan Price—who seeks to engage him as an equal.

Amid the constant drama of everyone vying for Dylan's approval (and failing to get it) are moments that resonate longer than any song. Example: In a crowded tour hotel room, Joan Baez sings one of her own compositions at the top of her lungs, while in the corner, oblivious, Dylan twitches in his chair, typing out a new song lyric while singing soundlessly to himself, alone in the universe he reigns.

Other recommended rentals directed by D. A. Pennebaker:
Monterey Pop

Don't Look Now

Eerie glam spookiness :**ATTITUDE**
Sexy supernatural thriller :**MOOD**

DIRECTOR: Nicolas Roeg (1973—U.K.)
CAST: Donald Sutherland, Julie Christie, Hilary Mason
IN ENGLISH; COLOR

It's a mystery, but the clues go in circles. It's a love story, but the lovers are doomed. It's suspenseful, but the worst has already happened. It's a tale of redemption, but the universe is godless. Adapting this elegant Daphne du Maurier short story (she also wrote *Rebecca*), comes director Nicolas Roeg (*Walkabout, The Man Who Fell to Earth*) at his peak. Mixing sex and mysticism, he uses Venice at its most beautiful and melancholy as a backdrop.

Donald Sutherland plays an arrogant, raffish architect with psychic gifts who denies his own powers. His grief-stricken wife, the ferocious Julie Christie, believes that their dead child is speaking to them from beyond the grave. Substituting faith in her own instincts for genuine second sight, she urges Donald to confront his gifts, his fears, and ultimately, the fate that awaits him for confusing the two.

Sutherland refuses until it's too late. Ego and vulnerability add depth to his portrayal of a man seeking refuge from his emotions in the stuff of men: work, sex, and minimizing the emotions of his wife. A key component of this ruthless portrait of the dumb-ass willfulness of husbands—no matter how smart they are—is that the wife usually knows better, even if she can't convince herself that she does. And in playing a character this vain, Sutherland shows no vanity as an actor. He doesn't try to make us like him.

Julie Christie never looked so fabulous, nor underplayed so powerfully. She and Sutherland share a famous nude love scene (often ranked as the hottest ever in a mainstream picture) that is the most accurate depiction of how adults actually make love yet filmed. And, unlike most love scenes, this one reveals much of the two characters even as it arouses. It also seems to appeal equally to men and to women.

Roeg's worldview may be steeped in dread, but he understands the denial of those who feel the proximity of the void, but refuse to acknowledge that they do. The story sees death and foreboding everywhere, and in Venice Roeg finds a city that reflects this view. His is not the sunny Venice of lovers, but a damp, grimy place, sensual and soaked in decay. Venice itself should serve as a warning, but Sutherland does not heed it.

Roeg, an editor of subtlety and daring, leaps backward and forward in time to suggest Sutherland's abilities to perceive the future, but still never neglects the tiny, everyday, sensual details: a shard of colored glass falling through space, the pattern spilled mustard makes across an ancient tile floor, the gleaming wake of a motorboat hearse cutting through the Venice canals.

A complex, creepy tale—the ending will scare you to death.

Other recommended rentals directed by Nicolas Roeg:
Bad Timing
The Man Who Fell to Earth
Performance (see page 129)

The Duellists

Affaire d'honneur **:ATTITUDE**
Action, costumes, candelit romance **:MOOD**

DIRECTOR: Ridley Scott 1977—U.K.)
CAST: Keith Carradine, Harvey Keitel, Albert Finney, Edward Fox
IN ENGLISH; COLOR

Back in Napoleon's time Keith Carradine—a French cavalryman—unknowingly insults Harvey Keitel—another French cavalryman who might just be a tad bit psychotic. Since this movie

Keith Carradine in *The Duellists*

is almost twenty years old, Keitel plays a more inward sort of psychotic; back then he could really *brood*. With gleeful psychotic abandon (the one thing Keitel's character enjoys is a good *hate*) Keitel challenges Carradine to a duel of honor, and the path of their lives is set. Both are career soldiers, both fight for Napoleon. There, similarities of luck, class, and politics end, and if you're versed in the history of the age no doubt there's all sorts of really swell references to historical events that will provide extra insight. But you don't have to know anything about history to enjoy the picture.

As their careers rise and fall, as Keith Carradine finds and loses love, as Harvey Keitel finds only increasing disappointment, the constant in their lives remains one another. They meet over and over, always by accident, fighting a battle that makes no sense, and is all the more compelling because. They fight with pistols, they fight with swords, they fight on horseback, on foot, in the fog, in the forest, in stables, in drawing rooms, and in the bright sunshine. They fight in secret and they fight with full military accompaniment. They fight with a realistic intent that speaks volumes about their training for the film.

Though it's difficult to believe that either could be French cavalry officers, Keitel and Carradine make superb antagonists. Keitel's pure New York, all neurosis and inner torment, while Carradine is the essence of the breezy, naturally fortunate West Coast. The director doesn't seem to give them much direction regarding character. Left to fend for themselves, and apparently unwilling to learn new accents, Keitel sounds like he's hailing a cab at Thoity-thoid 'n' Thoid, while Carradine speaks like the adenoidal Southern Californian he is.

This is Scott's debut (he later directed *Alien* and *Blade Runner*). Fresh from a career in English TV commercials, Scott was not quite up to dealing with the necessities of plot and character. He excels at odd things. He captures the varying moods of certain rooms, of men's clubs, of castles, and particularly the tortured, formal relations between men and women. He works hard to capture the light, the look, and the feel of the early 1800s. Sometimes you may be more aware of his working hard than of his getting it right.

Still, a gritty, if slightly overblown sense of realism emerges. The 1800s featured lots of dirt, apparently, and the duels themselves are glamorous, harrowing, and way cool. They function as a violent equivalent of music videos—short, self-contained explosions of creative energy—and are the high points of the film, where the director concentrated most of his attention.

The ending, which comes courtesy of the Joseph Conrad short story from which the film is adapted, will linger long after the credits roll. The finale also makes up for the film's flaws, which are minor: bad accents, slow patches, sentimentality. Another good date movie: horses, costumes, and candlelit kisses.

Other recommended rentals directed by Ridley Scott:
Alien
Blade Runner

Fearless

Life after death :**ATTITUDE**
Wrenching, uplifting drama :**MOOD**

DIRECTOR: Peter Weir (1993—U.S.A.)
CAST: Jeff Bridges, Rosie Perez, Isabella Rossellini
IN ENGLISH; COLOR

Jeff Bridges in *Fearless*

The least appreciated film of '93 follows Jeff Bridges and Rosie Perez (in an unexpectedly quiet, accurate, and affecting performance) as two survivors of a horrible airplane crash. Bridges goes slightly mad from his newfound absence of fear and Perez becomes slightly catatonic from her newfound absence of anything but.

From the exploration of their powerful bond as survivors arise the themes of responsibility, the limits of caring, and how one brief moment can completely alter what seemed to be lifelong values.

Few recent Hollywood films would attempt, much less pull off, this modern and complex a perspective. Director Peter Weir (*Dead Poets Society*) presents both our (useless) newfangled ideas about grief and its ages-old inescapable processes. Weir wastes no time explaining Bridges's spiritual confusion; he lets Bridges play out the madness. Bridges remains among the most likable and selfless of movie stars. He fearlessly displays his character's worst aspects: arrogance, insensitivity, panic, and selfishness.

Bridges cannot connect to his wife (Isabella Rossellini), ignores his son, and concentrates on Rosie Perez, whose baffled husband doesn't know what to make of this wealthy stranger in their midst. Weir does not shrink from questions of class; he makes plain how much easier it is for Bridges to wallow in his suffering. Perez, after all, has to get up in the midst of her sorrow and go to work.

Weir's quiet approach finds voice in the disavowel of sentimentality or easy answers. If mainstream audiences these days reject ambiguities, it's because today's directors are afraid to take them on. Weir, coming off of a series of successful formulaic mainstream pictures, captures the spirituality underlying bourgeois family life simply by depicting its rhythms with dispassionate accuracy. One stumbling conversation between Bridges and Rossellini speaks volumes about their marriage.

The crash remains a mystery until the final fifteen minutes, and then, in flashback, serves as the climax of the film. Weir doesn't try to build suspense; we all know the plane is going down. He focuses instead on the rituals of terror the doomed passengers perform. Their fear is all too real; this sequence is both horrible and eerily comforting. As the plane flies apart in slow motion, the film shifts into a trancelike state. A lesser director would have gone for big explosions and rapid-fire editing. Weir keeps it simple, quiet, and terrible. By presenting the crash with religious awe, he honors rather than exploits the deaths we see on-screen.

Weir's commitment to excellence is evident throughout: in the sets, the costumes, the supporting cast (Rossellini is particularly touching), the subtle music, and the inspired use of slow motion in the finale.

Bridges's and Perez's struggle to find life in the aftermath of death will move you to unsentimental, adult tears. This is a rare thing: a genuinely moving, insightful picture from a major modern studio.

Other recommended rentals directed by Peter Weir:
The Last Wave

A Fistful of Dynamite (aka Duck, You Sucker!)
Ka-boom! :ATTITUDE
Exciting, adorable spaghetti western :MOOD

DIRECTOR: Sergio Leone (1971—Italy)
CAST: James Coburn, Rod Steiger, Romolo Valli
IN ENGLISH; COLOR

This is Sergio Leone's (*The Good, the Bad, and the Ugly*) only western with no underlying cinematic mission, which makes it his most charming and most fun, in a brain-dead kind of way. Leone opts for a light opera of noise and laughter, featuring his usual slapstick violence, goopy sentimentality, outrageous humor, and atrocious dubbing. No matter how self-amused or relaxed the master stylist might be, he cannot make a graceless film.

Plot? There must be a plot in here someplace. . . . James Coburn plays a devil-may-care political revolutionary, an anti-English Irishman on the run in Mexico. There he discovers Rod Steiger, who—while speaking in the most unintentionally hilarious Mexican accent in cinema history—recruits Coburn to his cause, the Mexican revolution (and the robbing of rich folks in its name). Coburn's accent is no more firmly fixed than Steiger's, but it does occasionally resemble an Irish pattern. Steiger, at his best, sounds Italian. Steiger can be an annoying actor, and Leone lets him indulge in his most exasperating mannerisms. To enjoy the picture, one must forgive Steiger in advance.

Coburn plays a demolition expert, so he gets to blow things up. Coburn's entrance is immortal: a series of symmetrically timed, perfectly placed explosions erupt from either side of the roadway, and through their smoke appears Coburn, riding a turn-of-the-century motorcycle. Lots of things get blown up and lots of people get shot—all with those Leone guns that make that really strange *ppweew!* sound that only guns in Leone pictures make.

As usual, Leone holds his screen-filling close-ups forever, stages action sequences as opéra bouffe, employs Ennio Morricone for a sound track of musical grunts and whistles, lets the story lag shamefully at least twice, presents the bonding between men as the most important activity in life, and does his apparent best to kill several stuntmen by placing them in much too close proximity to the biggest on-screen explosions you ever saw, given the available pyrotechnics technology in 1971.

Steiger betrays Coburn a couple of times and vice versa, allowing Leone to work variations on his usual themes of trust and vengeance. If the plot and character development appear offhand, if the action in certain large-scale sequences is sloppy, it does nothing to lessen the fun. Even when Leone takes a working vacation—as he apparently did here—his editing, treatment of figures in a frame, use of sound track, romantic soul, and sheer exuberance remain wondrous and appealing.

Not the first western you might rent, and perhaps primarily for those who truly love westerns or Leone or even Coburn. This picture does not reward concentration; it's best enjoyed like a day on the river; let it drift by under your lazy gaze and be enchanted.

Other recommended rentals directed by Sergio Leone:
A Few Dollars More
A Fistful of Dollars
The Good, the Bad, and the Ugly
Once Upon a Time in America
Once Upon a Time in the West

A Flash of Green

Mood and sweat :**ATTITUDE**
John D. MacDonald thriller with a conscience :**MOOD**

DIRECTOR: Victor Nuñez (1984—U.S.A.)
CAST: Ed Harris, Richard Jordan, Blair Brown
IN ENGLISH; COLOR

A tough, smart little thriller set in go-go suburban Florida in the just-booming late 1950s. . . . Ed Harris plays a newspaperman who learns too much about his tiny town, about his place in it, and about his own values. Typical of John D. MacDonald, when our hero observes corruption in the world, he finds an equivalent of it within himself, usually illuminated by his response to what he uncovers. MacDonald heroes often discover themselves to be living in a glass house at which they must throw stones.

Ed Harris believes in progress, but from a distance. Reluctant to get involved, Harris hides behind his observer's role until forced to make a choice: to live with dishonesty and prosper, or to bring it to light and ruin his friends. At first he tries to do neither, and suffers the loss of love, respect, and, for a while, the use of both arms. Once Harris learns, to his surprise, that he's capable both of choice and of action, he almost relishes the dues he has to pay. They appear to him as absolution for his days of cowardice.

Richard Jordan, too overweight to be recognized as the former pretty-boy leading man he was, seems reluctant to shift from the overstuffed chair in his office. But when he does move, he projects menace aplenty. He never quite gets his Southern accent right, but his fleshy frame labels him as an icon of immorality. Jordan's real-life wife, Blair Brown, plays the woman whose admiration Harris wants more than anything. She radiates a "respectable" repressed sexuality just waiting to be unleashed. When Harris attempts to do so, he gets more than he can handle.

Director Nuñez captures MacDonald's saga of small-town dirty dealing and disappointing self-discovery a little too accurately; the film is as overlong, as overdetailed, as harum-scarum in character emphasis, and as lacking in climax as the book. Fortunately, it's also as sweaty, humid, frightening, and difficult to shake. The languid storytelling makes the frames seem static, but the camera moves constantly, snaking through the junglelike backyards and concrete seats of rural power like an all-seeing eye. For all of Nuñez's sensitivity, he knows how to structure mayhem; he never forgets that this is a thriller, however slowly paced. Nuñez understands MacDonald's Florida, which the author always painted as potential paradise spoiled by greedheads; a place in need of small men in small towns to stand in opposition to the march of progress. Nuñez has a feel for the light of Florida, for the weight of its heat and for the lust that springs up in the boredom of air-conditioned afternoons. He has a gift for atmosphere—moral, sexual, and political—that makes up for his shortcomings as a storyteller. Mac-Donald's plot is as convoluted as the choices his characters face, and a more narrative-oriented director might have neglected the tiny details that make the characters and situations seem so real.

49th Parallel

There Will Always Be an England :**ATTITUDE**
Stirring WWII action :**MOOD**

DIRECTOR: Michael Powell (1941—U.K.)
CAST: Leslie Howard, Anton Walbrook, Laurence Olivier, Eric Portman
IN ENGLISH; B/W

A submarine blasted out of an arctic bay, a murder at a lonely frontier outpost, a stolen airplane, a desperate chase across the length of Canada, Eskimos and Indians pursuing Nazis . . .

Masters of sophisticated perversity Michael Powell (director) and Emeric Pressburger (screenwriter) couldn't make a straightforward war movie if their lives depended on it. No, they had to undertake one of the most daring productions in British film history. First, they dragged an entire production company across the Atlantic Ocean, dodging German U-boats all the way. Then they managed fifty thousand miles of travel on a limited budget, shooting on location from Hudson Bay to Vancouver to the Canadian Rockies. They dared to present—in the midst of the war—an ineffectual Englishman played to effete perfection by Leslie Howard, and a sympathetic German soldier whose moving speech on behalf of anti-Hitler German refugees is delivered with inspirational sincerity by Anton Walbrook.

The result, an exemplary blend of entertainment and propaganda, secured Oscar nominations for Best Picture, won the Oscar for Best Original Story, and proved a smashing box-office success in America, grossing over five million. And, perhaps, swayed American public opinion toward favoring the war—which was why the British Ministry of Information bankrolled the film in the first place.

Powell and Pressburger's intelligence is evident in the brilliant dialogue, the high suspense of the chase, the masterful setting of each scene in a new location, the powerful action sequences, and the surprisingly effective finale. As elegant and stylized as the picture may be, modern it is not.

The cutting speed drags. The pacing is either just right or too slow, and the change from one to another is distracting. The episodic nature of the story—which follows fugitive Nazis as they travel across Canada—ensures that "chapters" are always beginning and ending, sometimes clumsily. Happily, the film's archaic aspect makes for relaxed viewing; you watch from a slight, bemused distance.

The characterizations suffer only from being designed as social archetypes. Each represents a different element included to teach a different patriotic lesson: the good German, the evil German, the withdrawn Englishman, the innocent girl. It's a finely drawn Brit version of the American GI picture, in which every infantry patrol features a Kowalski from Brooklyn, a farm boy, and a Harvard graduate.

Laurence Olivier plays the French-Canadian fur trapper Johnny. His performance at first seems ridiculous—due to his "Pepe Le Pew" *Franch* accent—but after the initial shock he proves quite touching. Eric Portman, as the Nazi leader, Hirth, is a classic movie Nazi: tireless, sinister, and contemptuous of all democracy. Glynis Johns plays Anna, the archetypal innocent young girl endangered by Nazi corruption. Always ready to sneak in forbidden eroticism, Powell guides Johns through a performance that's the essence of innocence verging on adult discovery.

The joys of this film almost contradict one another: thrilling action, intelligent dialogue, riveting chase scenes, and a revealing portrait of the filmmaking mentality of another era.

Other recommended rentals directed by Michael Powell and/or Emeric Pressburger:

Black Narcissus (see page 19)

I Know Where I'm Going (see page 68)

The Life and Times of Colonel Blimp

Peeping Tom (see page 127)

The Red Shoes

The Small Back Room

Thief of Bagdad (1940; see page 172)

Gates of Heaven

Strange Americana **:ATTITUDE**
Slow, garish, poetic documentary **:MOOD**

DIRECTOR: Errol Morris (1978—U.S.A.)
IN ENGLISH; COLOR

Errol Morris is the finest director of documentaries America has produced in the last twenty years. His films are like no others: alienated, lacking in narration or explanation, and always entertaining.

Gates is Morris's debut, and concerns a pet cemetery in central California. The superficial subject matter of Errol's films, whether pet cemeteries, miscarriages of justice (*The Thin Blue Line*), or the nature of the universe (*A Brief History of Time*), generates the forward momentum of the film, but the significant content lurks beneath our view, beyond our grasp. While *Gates* is hilarious, sad, and insightful as regards its subjects—the weird family who owns the cemetery and the sad sacks who bury their pets there—those subjects operate as metaphors for the tale Morris truly wants to tell.

Gates of Heaven is far from perfect. It's mean-spirited, exploitative of its subjects, too slow, too in love with its own style, and breaks the basic moral compact between the person in front of the camera and the person behind. But, *Gates* does offer humor, pathos, and an almost hallucinatory intimacy with its subjects. Morris, while happy to make us laugh, is aiming higher. He intended to make a straightforward film about a pet cemetery, but became enthralled with his subjects and their obsessive considerations of the most profound and unanswerable questions: What motivates the struggle to live? What occurs after death? How does one maintain faith when confronted with the finality of death?

The first section of the film (which crosscuts between three men who try to make a go of a pet cemetery and fail) is metaphorical of mankind struggling with purely secular concerns: money, ambition, success. The second section—one of the most extraordinary in documentary history—consists of a single, unbroken shot of an old lady as she sits in a wheelchair recounting her life's story. The naked intimacy of her confessions—both her knowing confession (what she says), and her unknowing confession (what we surmise about her from what she says)—will make you squirm in your seat, but you will be unable to look away.

The third section takes place at the pet cemetery and represents the striving after higher truths. It features a classic three-tiered holy hierarchy: the dad (who owns the place), the eldest son (a bit of a dolt), and the younger son (the enthusiastic heir apparent). The eldest son is the most memorable character in the film. For Morris, he represents the willfully ignorant undercurrent of the American Dream. Morris grants the eldest son little mercy, and lets him ramble on in his New Age success-speak until we all recognize that the guy has no idea what he's talking about.

Morris presents these "types" so that we can reflect on our own philosophical and spiritual struggles. His message is that everyone, no matter how poorly dressed, inarticulate, bumbling, or hopeless, reflects constantly on issues of faith. Their groping toward an answer is meant to mirror our own musings on the same questions. Morris is saying that these ridiculous figures are no more ridiculous than anybody else when it comes to riddles of faith. Their failed articulation merely reflects our own.

Heavy stuff, but always engaging. A quirky film; slow, hilarious, and rewarding. Shot in fantastically lurid colors and edited with a sure, steady hand—the pacing is like nothing you've ever seen.

Other recommended rentals directed by Errol Morris:

A Brief History of Time

The Thin Blue Line

Vernon, Florida (see page 178)

Hard-Boiled

Transcendent ultraviolence :ATTITUDE
Nonstop shoot-outs :MOOD

DIRECTOR: John Woo (1991—Hong Kong)
CAST: Chow Yun-Fat, Tony Leung
IN CANTONESE WITH ENGLISH SUBTITLES; COLOR

John Woo creates the most poetic, lyrical, technologically impossible, rhythmic, orgasmic, skillfully edited, widely imitated action sequences in the history of filmmaking. His work is a singular amalgam of classic cinema, primal bloodletting, emotional volatility, and cheesy cornball. Underlying the nonstop carnage is the unmistakable soul of an artist who chooses to express himself, on all issues and levels of profundity or its absence, in cinematic violence. The philosophical/moral/cosmic intricacies that Ingmar Bergman expressed by Death playing chess on the beach, John Woo discovers in the muzzle flash of a Glock-19. . . .

The plot moves quickly but makes little sense: Chow Yun-Fat, the Hong Kong heartthrob leading man of most Woo pictures, plays a hotheaded cop in the Dirty Harry mode. Tony Leung plays either a psycho gunrunning assassin or a psycho undercover cop pretending all too convincingly to be a gunrunning assassin. Yun-Fat and Leung chase each other around while killing everyone in sight, then they team up and kill everyone who was in hiding.

In the final sequence, Yun-Fat and Leung take on the evil head gunrunner, killing an army of gunmen while the bad guy blows up a hospital. This nonstop action sequence takes almost forty-five minutes. It grows continually more inventive and insane until the picture—and you, most likely—climax. It's the last ten minutes of *Zabriskie Point* meets *Die Hard* (a movie greatly influenced by earlier Woo work) meets *The Wild Bunch* (a major influence on Woo) meets the Hong Kong kung-fu aesthetic transferred to modern weaponry.

Amid the explosions, car crashes, and escalating body count are Woo's trademark sappy romance, weird homoeroticism, fetishistic love of lethal hardware, artistic slow motion, and mind-blowing editing.

Woo, a Cantonese-speaking Hong Kong Chinese by birth, finds

his inspiration in the cinema of the West. This is the last film he directed in Hong Kong before emigrating to the U.S. It's certainly his most "Western"; some see it as his audition for Hollywood. It features the most extended and complex (but least meaningful in a moral sense) of all his shoot-outs. The violence in Woo's pictures functions not only as his expression of the cinematic arts, but also, always, as metaphor. These astounding sequences announce the end of an era; Woo's mirror to the rising violence and chaos in Hong Kong as the Communist takeover of 1997 looms.

Despite the presumably limited range of colors in his palette, John Woo is not only a major and seldom-credited influence on every visual stylist who shoots an action sequence (not least among his admitted copiers: Luc Besson and Quentin Tarantino) but, to put it simply, a great and enduring artist. His understanding of pure cinema—that which can be expressed emotionally by a camera movement or an edit or a shift in motion speeds—has no equal among Western directors for all of their obsession with meaning.

Woo doesn't give two hoots for meaning, cogent narrative, or even rational sense. He wants emotion, and violence is how he gets it.

Other recommended rentals directed by John Woo:
A Better Tomorrow
Bullet in the Head
Hard Target
The Killer (see page 78)

Hell Is for Heroes
"The Gallant Men"—with a conscience :ATTITUDE
Action-packed infantry shoot-'em-up :MOOD

DIRECTOR: Don Siegel (1962—U.S.A.)
CAST: Steve McQueen, Fess Parker, Bob Newhart, James Coburn
IN ENGLISH; B/W

Nick Adams, Fess Parker, Steve McQueen, and Bobby Darin in *Hell Is for Heroes*

In his most committed performance, Steve McQueen gives a text-book rendition of simple psychopathy. His character blazes with hate, so removed from normal human interaction and so ready to kill that even the other members of his new infantry platoon fear him. Playing a shell-shocked, violence-ravaged veteran, McQueen brings deep layers of pain to a man who believes that he never betrays an emotion.

Maybe the once familiar plot and its concerns aren't so familiar anymore. It's been a long time since anyone made a nonironic war movie, much less a black-and-white picture about World War II. Director Don Siegel (*Dirty Harry*, 1956's *Invasion of the Body Snatchers*) turns the normal WWII infantry platoon conventions topsy-turvy. Yes, the platoon features a variety of types: Fess Parker as the steady sergeant, James Coburn as the brainy Southerner, Bobby Darin as a streetwise hustler, and Harry Guardino as the sagelike older vet. Even semi–teen throb Nick Adams is tossed into the mix as a lovable Polish refugee.

Unlike most movie platoons, however, these guys all loathe one another, and they care for McQueen even less. Moreover, when the platoon is called upon to stand its ground and repel a German advance of overwhelming numerical superiority, no one wants to be a hero. Everyone except McQueen wants to run away as fast as he can. McQueen just wants to kill people. If they happen to be German, swell.

For a film made in 1962, *Hell* seems a remarkable precursor to the grunts' attitude toward war in Vietnam. Cynical, revisionist, and anti-heroic, Siegel sought to annihilate every WWII movie convention except the love of action. Between McQueen's alienated, blank-faced nonconformist and Siegel's spare, bitter tone, the film's intent—if not its plot—seems remarkably hip.

Though there are some overlong lulls between bouts of combat—lulls padded with Bob Newhart comedy routines and Bobby Darin crooning over a guitar—when the combat returns, the action more than justifies the waiting. Siegel functions in a pre-Peckinpah universe: He has neither slow motion nor blood-bags, but he knows how to stage brutal, exciting battles.

Siegel employs two visual modes: disinterested and TV-like for exposition, rhythmic and imaginative when people kill each other. He brings a definite Peckinpah glee to movie bloodletting, a glee that serves as a reflection of the soldier's joyous catharsis in the moment of murder. The positively sexual charge that McQueen gets out of gunning down Jerries—and McQueen packs one of the most Freudian machine guns in war movie–hero history—only intensifies the sadistic undertone.

And after all the character building, sexy shoot-outs, and lame humor interludes, it turns out Siegel isn't making a nihilistic gorefest, but a message picture. The message? Not War Is Hell, or even War Is a Tragic Waste of Human Life, but: All Effort Goes for Naught, which is a pretty happening message for 1962.

That's right, Siegel took McQueen, a penis-substitute machine gun, and Bobby Darin, threw them together and came up with the myth of Sisyphus. What perversity! Who else would dare? The shocking transition from heroic action to chilling message has no equivalent in the war-movie genre. The final five minutes are absolutely astonishing.

Uneven, enthralling, and unique—not one minute of romance, not one woman in the plot, and very little appeal for women, period (except as a study of the violent impulses of men). Otherwise, a genre treasure, the last of its kind, a thinking war movie.

Other recommended rentals directed by Don Siegel:
Invasion of the Body Snatchers (1956)

Henry V

We happy few **:ATTITUDE**
Cheery, colorful Shakespeare **:MOOD**

DIRECTOR: Laurence Olivier (1944—U.K.)
CAST: Laurence Olivier, Robert Newton, Leslie Banks
IN ENGLISH; TECHNICOLOR

Laurence Olivier as Henry V

Another stellar piece of propaganda to cheer the Brits during the final days of the war. No Englishman ever won a bigger battle against a stronger enemy than Henry V, so he's the perfect unifying hero to rally a nation. Henry's also a good subject for Olivier's directorial debut; he's not a character—he's a speechifier, and nobody delivers those speeches like Olivier.

The play is presented in bright, cheery Technicolor, with the back-grounds deliberately cartoony and theatrical. The trees are rounded green lollipops, the sky a surreal blue. As usual with the Technicolor of this era, the greens and reds pop off the screen, especially in laser-disc format. Olivier directs simply, with lots of close-ups of his noble face and his bottomless, glittering eyes.

The one stirring moment of pure cinema occurs in the first few min-utes, when we leave the Globe Theatre for the battlefield of Agincourt. The transition from one to another is magical, and marks Olivier's de-liberate acknowledgment of the gulf between film and theater. Rec-ognizing the difference—for England's most renowned Shakespearean stage actor and hence the embodiment of all English snobberies about the sanctity of the stage in general and Shakespeare in particular—was a conscious act of pragmatism and humility.

By way of contrast, consider the Shakespeare cinema of Kenneth Branagh, in which the camera functions as a movable stage: all the ac-tion occurs dead center on the screen. Branagh sets his scenes as if for the stage and then points a camera. Olivier adapted Shakespeare for the screen. If his images are sometimes too formal or sometimes too playful, at least he tries.

By calling attention to the movieness of his construction, and by delivering his speeches in big, lip-reading close-ups, Olivier took an-other step in the direction of his audience: He turns Shakespeare pop. Olivier wants to make it easy for his audience to understand the Bard. He creates a Shakespeare that works as a classic, but also succeeds as popular entertainment.

Orson Welles's Shakespeare films—the gloomy *Macbeth* or *Othello*—stand as monuments, but they're almost unwatchable for their self-conscious grandiosity and sleep-inducing, shadowy framing. Welles insists that we know that *he* knew that he was dealing with the classics. "Classic" meant ponderous and slow. Olivier, conversely, in-sists that mass entertainment need not be stupid and that the Bard need not be inaccessible. Where others deliver scenery-rattling pro-nouncements from dark corners, Olivier plays dress-up in a glisten-ing, happy, artificial universe, making himself more heroic by his accessibility, and giving his audience a genuine escape from the dreary wartime reality waiting outside the theater.

Excellent Shakespeare for kids, with magnificent Technicolor, consistently imaginative costumes, and Olivier's technically perfect, infinitely shaded, and loving oratory.

Other recommended rentals directed by Laurence Olivier:
Richard III (1955)

The Hit

Grace under pressure **:ATTITUDE**
Languid gangster road movie **:MOOD**

DIRECTOR: Stephen Frears (1984—U.K.)
CAST: Terence Stamp, John Hurt, Tim Roth, Bill Hunter, Fernando Rey
IN ENGLISH; COLOR

An English contrary suspense thriller with a snitch for a hero, a hit man for an antihero, and the hallmarks of a road movie—lovely, full-frame landscapes coupled with a solemn sense of the passing of time—and a very nasty sense of humor.

Terence Stamp, looking impossibly beatific, plays a gangster-turned-informer hiding in Spain ten years after he ratted out his mobster boss. John Hurt, appearing nerve-wracked and satanic, plays a hit man assigned to kidnap Stamp to Paris for the mobster's revenge. Hurt's assistant is Tim Roth as a bungling, impulsive assassin-in-training. Once kidnapped, Stamp doesn't seem too worried. He's been doing a lot of reading about the nature of death, he says, and has no fear of The End. The hit man, having seen (many) others in similar situations, remains unconvinced. "Wait till it really happens," Hurt says, "and see how you react." So we do. . . .

Hurt and Roth stagger around Spain with Stamp in tow, lurching from misadventure to screw-up. These misadventures, though unusual for a gangster movie, seem real enough to anyone who has ever had an important errand and finds that events won't cooperate. Even the most exotic jobs (like that of hit man) run afoul of the most mundane problems.

Director Frears (*Dangerous Liaisons*) revels in the big frame of the movies after his years directing television. He fills the screen from top to bottom with the blue Spanish sky and the vast Spanish plains, across which flies the tiny car containing the three men. Frears uses the same big-screen approach inside the car, blasting close-ups like Sergio Leone. And, like Leone, Frears cuts from wide-open landscape shots to huge full-face close-ups. It's a powerful technique.

It's not that the picture resembles a western so much as the characters behave as if they were living through one, especially Tim Roth. Hurt just wants to do his job, but Roth and Stamp are too aware of their mythic, highly charged situation (killer and victim in close proximity) and both keep trying to be larger than life. Hurt, like a deadly mother hen, wearily reminds them of the dreariness of their circumstances. Even though Roth is going to shoot Stamp, they become secret allies, almost pals. Hurt notes this breach of hit-man decorum with understated alarm.

Underplaying is John Hurt's métier and he makes the most of his opportunities to do or say nothing. His stillness carries considerable import; it's sinister as hell. Hurt finds trouble only when he succumbs to a merciful urge. Stamp has problems when the end comes sooner than he expects, and Roth learns that perhaps he should try another profession.

The thrills are in the acting, the hilarious arguments, and the constant shifting tensions between the men. Those shifts are caused by a young Spanish beauty whom they snatch as a hostage, and by Stamp's increasingly irritating serenity in the face of certain death. Hurt argues with Roth, Roth chases the girl while befriending Stamp, and Stamp watches it all unfold, smirking like a Zen monk. . . . When the big moment comes, will he crack?

Witty, graphically violent and featuring a distinctive visual style, an elegant sound track by Eric Clapton, and a moving tribute to John Lennon.

Other recommended rentals directed by Stephen Frears:

Bloody Kids
Dangerous Liaisons
The Grifters
My Beautiful Laundrette
The Snapper

Hombre

Paul Newman western **:ATTITUDE**
Talky, sunlit "message" western **:MOOD**

DIRECTOR: Martin Ritt (1966—U.S.A.)
CAST: Paul Newman, Martin Balsam, Richard Boone, Fredric March
IN ENGLISH; COLOR

Paul Newman in *Hombre*

Paul Newman utilizes a secret weapon in his attempt to make a Steve McQueen movie: novelist Elmore Leonard (*Get Shorty*). Leonard wrote several superb paperback westerns, including the novel on which this hard-as-nails screenplay is based. Leonard's cynical view of human nature finds expression in a western devoted to corruption, racism, and betrayal. These subjects, though typical of a rain-soaked, shadowy noir, are displayed for maximum contrast in the harsh, blinding sunshine of the desert Southwest.

Newman works hard to produce the wry world-weariness that Mc-Queen could do in his sleep; this seems to be Newman's warm-up for *Cool Hand Luke.* Here he plays "Luke" as a blue-eyed Apache, that is, as a white man raised by Indians. Hombre's Apache upbringing has taught him to be contemptuous of the hypocrisy of white society and to kill without its hypocritical notions of fair play. The whites who discover his mixed blood first throw him out of their stagecoach (racism), and then demand that he protect them from a gang of killers (hypocrisy).

Protect them he does, but the more he learns of his companions— an embezzling banker on the run, a cowardly boy, a slutty newlywed wife, an earthy widow—the more he experiences a curious duality: He dislikes them, but wants their approval. No matter that the sensible course is to leave them to die; he can't do it. In becoming "civilized," he's lost the ability to protect himself from loneliness.

This will lead him, at the climactic moment, to act more like a sentimental white man than is good for him. The screenplay regards this shift in character as a maturing, no matter what the final cost to Hombre. You may find it hilariously misguided.

Leonard creates a mélange of themes. Hombre embodies the rootless wanderer of John Ford westerns: the outsider yearning for a community that would never accept him as a member and whose restrictions he knows he couldn't bear. Another theme is the noir outsider who, because he is on the outside, clearly sees the hypocrisy of society, but is seduced by its comforts nonetheless. This downright weird combination allows *Hombre* to transcend both the genre (Paul Newman movies, not westerns) and its own weaker moments.

The supporting cast, anchored by the unholy Richard Boone as the lead villain, features mainstays Fredric March and Martin Balsam. Leonard's script gives Boone free rein to display all his pockfaced evil. Boone smiles a secret inner smile at his own portrayal; he's having lots of fun.

Director Martin Ritt gives Newman the star treatment, with lots of steely-eyed close-ups. He uses strange but very effective visuals for the desert exteriors. Ritt shoots long, curious angles, with folks crammed into the corner in the foreground looking way up at other folks standing off in the background. It's almost arty, and contrasts with his Cinemascope portrait shots of a stagecoach robbery and of the cast holed up in the abandoned mine.

The film's power lies in its slow, careful construction. Though it's often broadcast by some superstation, all chopped up by commercials, that's no way to appreciate the calculated rhythms of Leonard's story. The tension in Newman's portrayal matches the building tensions of the script, and delivers strong, old-fashioned western satisfaction.

Fine gunfights, amusing, mock-insightful dialogue, and a really enjoyable bad guy. Oh, and Paul Newman.

Other recommended rentals directed by Martin Ritt:
The Spy Who Came in from the Cold (see page 157)

Homicide

Existential cops & self-discovery :**ATTITUDE**
Intellectual cop movie :**MOOD**

DIRECTOR: David Mamet (1990—U.S.A.)
CAST: Joe Mantegna, William H. Macy, Ving Rhames
IN ENGLISH; COLOR

A two-headed beast of emotional/intellectual complexity and power, half cop movie, half brutal journey of self-knowledge, *Homicide* remains the most accurate film on race relations in America yet made, and a thorough exploration of the theme of achieved identity. It's also a totally satisfying *policier*, with villains, suspense, and violent, cop-movie action.

Joe Mantegna in *Homicide*

Though a cynical, well-executed thriller in dialogue, plot, and attitude, *Homicide* is after bigger game. David Mamet—award-winning playwright of *Speed the Plow* and *Oleanna*—uses the world of cops to explore the themes that intrigue him: What gives us our sense of belonging? To what or to whom do we owe loyalty? Is it possible to render real change without suffering tragic, crippling loss? Can Americans escape identities of class, race, work, or religion?

Mamet regular Joe Mantegna plays a man who believes himself to be all cop, until he's trapped in a situation that demands he choose between cop loyalty and what he perceives as loyalty to his true, long-denied self. It's the classic film noir dilemma in a thoroughly modern noir.

Homicide follows the noir conventions: Its protagonist is a man misunderstood, a man who lives by his own moral code, a code that provides the core of a self-invented identity. When this protective, identifying code breaks down, our hero must take his fate into his own hands, blaze his own trail for good or ill. Will his independence bring reward or punishment? That's the noir question. . . .

Mamet delivers this existential message undiluted: We make our own moral choices and for those choices, large and small, dues must be paid. The price our hero pays will mark him for the rest of his life. And, his insights regarding the difference between who he thinks he is and who events reveal him to be, will be neither pleasant nor life-affirming.

Mamet's hypernaturalist dialogue, all stops and starts and weird, fragmented phrases, is intended to remind us how difficult is *any* communication; how different in-groups create their own speech—both to protect their identity from outsiders and to reinforce their bond within the group; and to demonstrate how, in the "world of men," obliqueness is all. None of Mamet's characters ever say anything as direct as "I love you"; though they may say, "I'll rip your fucking heart out!" and mean "I love you." His characters' determination to never say what they mean forces the viewer to pay strict attention to every nuance. This adds to the considerable suspense.

Mamet's actors seldom use wild gestures; they speak slowly and clearly, they move with deliberation. Their performances, like Mamet's camera work, are understated to the point of invisibility. You may find this style slightly off-putting at first, but after a few minutes it becomes remarkably familiar.

A harrowing, suspenseful mixture of cop stuff and philosophy, one of the Ten Best Films of 1990 and one of the sadly neglected films of the last decade.

Other recommended rentals directed and/or written by David Mamet:

House of Games (see page 67)

Things Change

The Untouchables (1987, screenwriter)

House of Games

Existential con games & self-discovery **:ATTITUDE**

Slow, smart psychological suspense **:MOOD**

DIRECTOR: David Mamet (1987—U.S.A.)

CAST: Lindsay Crouse, Joe Mantegna, Ricky Jay, J.T. Walsh

IN ENGLISH; COLOR

Lindsay Crouse plays a rich, nosy, successful shrink suffering a vague existential malaise. By a plot convention not worth relating, she falls into the world of con men, here presented with documentary realism, as reflects Mamet's love for hustle-derived scenes. Joe Mantegna plays the seductive, ruthless, street-smart leader of the con men. One look into his baby-browns and Lindsay is hooked. Her attraction is more than sexual: Joe's reality represents all that Lindsay's safe, intellectual existence does not. Also—and this is never incidental for Mamet—she's upper class searching for real experience; he's working class looking for a way out.

As she moves deeper into this forbidden—and by definition antibourgeois—territory, Lindsay's heretofore suppressed dark and spontaneous side emerges. She finds her new self damned attractive. As have few Mamet heroes, she thrives in a strange new world, and happily casts off the baggage of her previous life.

But since *she* doesn't suffer from her transition, everyone else must, and, boy, do they. . . . Undertones of class war: When the working class act as they please, they hurt no one but themselves. When the rich attempt to emulate, in their fumbling, confused, and guilt-ridden fashion, the damage gets scattered indiscriminately.

Mamet's direction compels his characters to speak in flat, uninflected tones. Whether this reflects the director's clinical dispassion regarding (wo)man's folly, his excess of irony, or his newcomer's lack of assurance (this is Mamet's directorial debut), the effect can be plenty annoying, but only for about twenty minutes. When the plot kicks in you won't care how the characters speak.

Aside from turning down their personalities to the lowest possible volumes, the acting is superb. Crouse plays repression almost too well. Her character doesn't know what she feels until the moment is past; at first it seems she never responds to *anything,* but as the film progresses it's clear that her character refuses—until the climactic moment—to rely on instinct. She observes herself at a distance before she ever (re)acts. Mantegna's natural ease and apparent unself-consciousness amaze, as usual. The masterful sleight-of-hand magician Ricky Jay cameos as a menacing con man, while J. T. Walsh is as cynical and nasty as ever.

Mamet's con men con Crouse and they con us as well. We follow the action through her eyes, and anything she can't figure out, we can't. The tricky plot layers false clues on top of misdirection—as all good cons should—and builds wondrous suspense, especially given the calm, intelligent tone. Mamet seems equally interested in the psychodynamics of the con—the mutual seduction between conner and victim, the righteous ruthlessness of the con man, his insight into greed—and in the stripping away of illusions required to fully understand the dark side of the self. Combining the two in one film is a tall order. Mamet's cool, distanced approach works better when showing off the con than when delving into emotion, but it's his vision, and he makes it work.

Other recommended rentals directed and/or written by David Mamet:
Homicide (see page 65)
Things Change
The Untouchables (1987, screenwriter)

I Know Where I'm Going

Sweet corniness **:ATTITUDE**
Charming adult love story **:MOOD**

DIRECTORS: Michael Powell, Emeric Pressburger (1945—U.K.)
CAST: Wendy Hiller, Roger Livesey, Pamela Brown
IN ENGLISH; B/W

Wendy Hiller in *I Know Where I'm Going*

Why is it that the most hardened cynics make the sweetest romantics?

Masters of subtextual perversity Michael Powell and Emeric Pressburger (*The Red Shoes, Black Narcissus*) throw themselves wholeheartedly into a simple, patriotic love story. Written with unironic tenderness and verve, the plot follows Wendy Hiller as a headstrong young city girl come to a magical Scottish isle to marry an older man—a harrumphing, shallow businessman. (In keeping with Powell's mischievous sense of humor, her betrothed never appears on-screen.) While waiting for her fiancé to show up, Hiller falls, against her pragmatic judgment, for the local impoverished Scots lord.

Fate—in the form of bad weather—keeps Hiller from her intended, giving her newfound romance time to flourish. Powell/Pressburger hint that Celtic magic may be altering the natural world to guide Wendy in the proper direction. The directors show a touching joy at turning their misanthropic spirits to such a gentle, happy tale.

But this is not an entirely innocent romance. The film was released in 1945; Wendy's pluck and good humor are intended to inspire the home folks who have suffered through six years of blackouts and rationed petrol. Powell/Pressburger wanted to engage their action-sated audience and were not about to rehash their earlier work (*49th Parallel*). Changing their subject matter from war guys to women back home, they still delivered the necessary let's-all-pull-together encouragement.

However different their method, their message remains unchanged from *49th Parallel:* There will always be an England, and proof can be found in England's endlessly repeating order-maintaining rituals. Wendy Hiller's rejecting the rich old fart for the dashing, impoverished lord—despite her modern, independent-gal politics—demonstrates that war aside, determined young girls are still out there following their hearts. Her choice of "the Laird" also makes the point that the traditional ways, however lacking in material excess, are more desirable and honorable than grubbing after money.

When directors so worldly succumb so happily to corniness, why should we resist? Given the dark sensibility that lies at the heart of their other work, their sentimental enthusiasm for this deceptively simple tale seems a major affirmation. It's nice to experience old-fashioned cornball without the usual accompanying stupidity. What should be nothing more than a lesson in British wartime filmmaking becomes a little-known classic, a grown-up love story: engaging, poignant, and magical.

Other recommended rentals directed by Michael Powell and/or Emeric Pressburger:

In a Lonely Place

Heartbreaking noir :ATTITUDE
Damn smart adult suspense :MOOD

DIRECTOR: Nicholas Ray (1950—U.S.A.)
CAST: Humphrey Bogart, Gloria Grahame, Frank Lovejoy
IN ENGLISH; B/W

Gloria Grahame, Humphrey Bogart, and Frank Lovejoy in *In a Lonely Place*

Humphrey Bogart plays a screenwriter with a dangerous, perhaps murderous, temper. Acting on a whim, Gloria Grahame, playing an actress, provides him with an alibi when he's charged with murder. They try to fall in love, but Bogart's jealous insecurity conflicts with Grahame's sincere if matter-of-fact method of demonstrating her affection. In the mode of classic tragedy, Bogart's growing need for Grahame only makes him doubt her fidelity all the more. His jealousy fuels his temper, and as Grahame sees the extent of Bogart's inner rage, she begins to doubt his innocence. Grahame seeks to withdraw, and Bogart becomes more convinced that she'll betray him. In perfect synchronicity, the two avidly construct the walls of their own doomed fortresses, as only adults can.

All this is played out under the constant, looming cloud of Hollywood's unrelenting, no-middle-ground of soaring success or crushing failure. Accordingly, when Bogart's and Grahame's characters act against their hearts' best interests, director Ray is careful to portray their mistakes in career terms as well, since in the movie business it's often impossible to separate the two. The result is the most accurate treatise on emotional self-destruction and the social patterns of Hollywood—two not entirely unrelated subjects—ever made.

The unobtrusive black-and-white camera work grows increasingly claustrophobic, presenting each player as trapped in the world he or she has made. This visual sense of the walls closing in contributes to the potent suspense that fuels the second half of the film. Bogart and Grahame turn to love to escape the unpleasant patterns of their lives, but force of habit proves too much for both of them. Bogart's habit of suspicion and Grahame's of forgiveness should dovetail perfectly, but instead they cancel each other out. It's almost too real.

As are the easy humor, the accurate barroom banter, the deep silences of both affection and (later) hostility between Grahame and Bogart. Bogart underplays to perfection, and his rages spring to the surface with a terrifying and entirely believable energy. Grahame seems completely insane. Her singular combination of vulnerability, bulletproofness, and resigned willingness to accept the demons in herself and in others could only have been drawn from her by a director of uncommon sensitivity. Grahame and Nicholas Ray were husband and wife when this film was made. If Ray couldn't understand her, who could? This is Grahame's finest hour, the performance that solidified her legend.

And throughout, the underlying psychological tension of the love story does nothing to lessen the suspense of the murder mystery. Each subplot only makes the other stronger, because among the many virtues of this purely American masterpiece is the flawless structure of Andrew Solt's screenplay. He and Nicholas Ray build a modern tragedy out of modern materials: alienation, self-created distrust, and a willful refusal to believe in the unscheduled arrival of good news.

Other recommended rentals directed by Nicholas Ray:

Bigger Than Life (see page 17)

Johnny Guitar

Rebel Without a Cause

In Which We Serve

Rule Britannia! :**ATTITUDE**
Understated, character-driven war movie :**MOOD**

DIRECTORS: Noel Coward, David Lean (1942—U.K.)
CAST: Noel Coward, John Wills, Bernard Miles
IN ENGLISH; B/W

A dauntingly grammatical title for a thoroughly class act. While Americans were being goaded into a patriotic fervor by simpleminded fare like John Wayne in *Flying Tigers*, the English enjoyed more subtle, complex pro-war programming. Three other enduring English wartime films—*Henry V*, *I Know Where I'm Going*, and *49th Parallel*—are included in this book. While they are very much of their time, and have much to tell us about that era, fifty years later they all stand on their own as entertainment.

English playwright Noel Coward teamed with director David Lean (*Lawrence of Arabia, Brief Encounter, The Bridge on the River Kwai*) in this, Lean's directorial debut (though he shared director's credits with Coward). Lean also edited the film. His camera work grants the picture a visual elegance seldom seen in war movies. The jarring simplicity of the action sequences—which rely heavily on intercutting 16-mm footage from real battles—must be chalked up to real-world concerns. That is, neither money nor Nazi-free oceans existed for the staging of detailed movie battles. In this action picture, which offers plenty of battles, action is not the point.

The film is subtitled *The Story of a Ship*, and so we follow the British destroyer *Torrin* from the beginning of the war. Coward plays Commander Kinross, a character based on British war hero Lord Mountbatten, whose adventures while commanding a destroyer against the Germans inspired the story. Kinross's deadpan, quietly inspirational speeches to his crew are taken word-for-word from Mountbatten's.

The story follows the home life of several crew members who reside at tellingly different points along the ruthless British class continuum. Coward explains nothing, and so the dialogue, manners, and clothing of each crew member serve as our guide to their place in the social hierarchy. Detailing this hierarchy with care, Coward delivers the message that all classes must pull together to achieve victory. His delicacy and effectiveness in promulgating this message is the most striking aspect of the picture. And since Coward is more comfortable depicting emotions than managing action set pieces, the captain's speeches to his crew are more moving than ten German warplanes going down in flames. Lean and Coward's rigorous English understatement makes for rather slow pacing, and forces the modern viewer to concentrate on the all-critical details or fall asleep. Never a voice is raised, never a plot point is overemphasized, never anything so gaudy as an overdone action sequence is permitted to ruffle the calm, smooth tone. This built-in sense of assurance seems designed to help keep wartime audiences relaxed, and to remind them that no matter what the state of things at sea, at home Britain endures as always.

A war film for men and women; men will cry over all the guys-together heroism, women for the home-front heartbreak.

Other recommended rentals directed by David Lean:
The Bridge on the River Kwai
Brief Encounter
Great Expectations
Lawrence of Arabia
Oliver Twist

Jimi Hendrix

The one and only :ATTITUDE
Trippy, guitar-fueled documentary :MOOD

DIRECTORS: Joe Boyd, John Head, Gary Weiss (1973—U.S.A.)
CAST: Jimi Hendrix, Eric Clapton, Mick Jagger
IN ENGLISH; COLOR

Rendered extraordinary by carefully chosen concert footage and the prescience of its interview subjects, this is a straightforward, unsentimental study of Hendrix, his music, and the era from which it sprang.

Legendary scenemaker, record-label owner, and record producer Joe Boyd intercuts between Hendrix's sweet dad, three different girlfriends, various band members, a major with whom Hendrix served in the 101st Airborne, Little Richard, Pete Townshend of The Who, Eric Clapton, Mick Jagger, Lou Reed, Hendrix's road manager, and two of Hendrix's pals.

The pals and the first girlfriend speak with a rollicking, streetwise energy, spewing a mind-bending mixture of startling perception, 1960s claptrap, and genuinely intriguing—if completely idiotic—theorizing about life, death, and cosmic virtue. Along with footage of Hendrix's culture-clash appearance on *The Dick Cavett Show*, these friends provide the most compelling background to Jimi's life. While trying to suss out the wisdom from the bullshit, it helps to remember that in the era/lifestyle documented, folks smoked an awful lot of marijuana.

The 1970s hairdos, clothing, and conversational mannerisms may weaken the interviewees' credibility at first. But their loving, common-sense appreciation of Hendrix's apparently complex and evasive soul proves admirable and endearing. Everyone interviewed, even those with the most crass and exploitative views of Hendrix, speaks of his musical gifts with religious awe. The concert footage induces a similar feeling.

Jimi rips it up at Monterey Pop, the Isle of Wight Festival, Woodstock, live on British television, and incredibly, at Fillmore East in the sole appearance—the New Year's Eve debut and finale—of Hendrix's Band of Gypsies.

This concert, shot in black-and-white video, shows Hendrix at the height of his powers. The most unexpected and revealing performance, however, is a more simple affair. Hendrix sits alone on an all-white soundstage, dressed in his usual dazzling costume, playing a gigantic acoustic twelve-string guitar—is there anything as rare as footage of Hendrix playing acoustic?

Hendrix plays two slow blues numbers, demonstrating that in addition to his mastery of noise, distortion, and feedback, he was a virtuoso of sensitivity and feeling. The performance is riveting and alone justifies the price of rental. The other concert footage suffers only from the documentary style of the time: prolonged close-ups of Hendrix's face or his hands. Needless to say, his Woodstock rendition of "The Star-Spangled Banner" remains the ultimate electric guitar statement, a utilization of the mundane to achieve the visionary on a par with John Coltrane's "My Favorite Things."

The concerts are arrayed chronologically, so Hendrix changes from a wild-eyed, excited pup—all stage moves and audience chatter—to a distant master, indifferent to the crowd, lost and focused in a world of his own devising. It's an impressive and frightening transition from boy to man, from genius to god.

Boyd's editing produces a clear and scary picture of Hendrix's world. Cutting from those who loved him to those who exploited him to those who never understood him for a moment, Boyd shows the pressures on Hendrix, not the least of which was that everyone around Hendrix found him a defining figure. The cutting is intuitive, and the story revealed, complex. This is not a straightforward history or coronation, like The Who's *The Kids Are Alright,* but an attempt to address fame, money, groupies, race, professional respect/jealousy, drugs, and ambition, all in the context of one artist striving to be at one with his art. Boyd reminds us that the world outside the artist shapes him as much as his own artistic impulses. That may sound like a puny revelation, but in the universe of mythifying rock documentaries, such a perspective is practically revolutionary.

Two of the concert pieces run long, otherwise the structure and pace are perfect. Play it loud.

Juggernaut

> *Bomb-defusion spectacular* :ATTITUDE
> *Intelligent suspense thriller* :MOOD

DIRECTOR: Richard Lester (1974—U.K.)
CAST: Richard Harris, Omar Sharif, David Hemmings, Roy Kinnear, Anthony Hopkins
IN ENGLISH; COLOR

Richard Harris plays a champion bomb defuser, Omar Sharif the captain of a bomb-infested ocean liner, Anthony Hopkins the quiet cop from Scotland Yard, and I can't tell you which stalwart of the English stage plays the mad bomber—that might lessen the suspense. It may sound like *The Poseidon Adventure* goes tea-and-crumpets, and indeed, *Juggernaut* hails from the height of the 1970s disaster movie. Which perhaps explains why this literate, cynical gem never succeeded in America.

Richard Lester (*Help!*) brings his offhand visual style, his love of ambient sound, and his remarkable gift for directing actors. Richard Harris actually understates and David Hemmings (*Blow-Up*) actually gives a performance. Lester mocks Omar Sharif's cigar-store-Indian emotional range even as he exploits it, and the always reliable Roy Kinnear provides plenty of low-key (English) goofball humor.

Or as much humor as the plot allows. Seems someone has planted seven high-tech bombs on board the ocean liner *Britannic.* Only one man in the Empire can defuse them, and since this is an action thriller (however understated) he has to parachute out of an airplane into raging seas to do so. Once on board he must contend with every trick the devilish bomber conjures up, and that's plenty. Meanwhile, back on shore, Anthony Hopkins searches for clues high and low. Ian Holm (the android in *Alien*)—locked in a death-struggle with Hopkins over who can understate more cryptically—plays the conscience-stricken head of the cruise-ship company. On board, twelve hundred passengers suffer stoically as only the English of 1974 might: Not one threatens a lawsuit for stress or emotional suffering.

At the heart of the action, suspense, and, yes, comedy lie the bombs themselves. The documentary-realism Lester brings to the inner workings of these fiendish devices perfectly contrasts Harris's don't-give-a-shit attitude toward the very life he should be most interested in saving: his own. Harris may be offhand about the bombs, but Lester is deadly serious, and moves his camera ingeniously to provide a constantly compelling view of the defusing action.

The suspense lags only during the slightly overdone jump-from-the-airplane-climb-into-the-ship sequence. Lester never did well with mechanical stuff—unlike most modern directors, he prefers human beings.

And just because it's about bombs doesn't make *Juggernaut* a boys-only adventure. There are two well-drawn women characters and a romantic subplot that's modern in the extreme: It concerns affectionate but alienated lovers.

Wouldn't you love to bite your nails with suspense while never thinking for a moment that the picture is dumber than you are?

Other recommended rentals directed by Richard Lester:
A Hard Day's Night
Help!

Robin and Marian (see page 143)
The Three Musketeers (1974)

The Killer

Sentimental ultraviolence :**ATTITUDE**
Strange romantic nonstop shoot-outs :**MOOD**

DIRECTOR: John Woo (1989—Hong Kong)
CAST: Chow Yun-Fat, Danny Lee, Sally Yeh
AVAILABLE EITHER DUBBED IN ENGLISH, OR IN CANTONESE
WITH ENGLISH SUBTITLES; COLOR

Leading man Chow Yun-Fat plays a modern version of a wushu knight, the stylish, unruffled hero of Chinese myth. Yun-Fat, a ruthless hit man, is pursued by his alter ego, Danny Lee, a cop first obsessed with apprehending Fat, and then obsessed with protecting him. Their link? A nightclub singer inadvertently blinded during one of Fat's hits. The two men begin as deadly enemies, recognize their bond as men of violence, and end as blood brothers.

Chow Yun-Fat is the true James Bond. No one in screen history has handled a pistol so smoothly nor kept his suit so unwrinkled in the midst of carnage. Wielding two pistols in a manner imitated by Stallone, Willis, Van Damme, or any action hero you can name, Yun-Fat is as evenhanded as a spider. He keeps a crooked grin on his face and a cigarette dangling from his mouth. His attitude, style, and savoir faire are taken from the French film star Alain Delon, in particular Delon's role in Jean-Pierre Melville's seminal noir, *Le Samourai,* a Woo favorite.

As one expects with Woo, the plot is incomprehensible. Though dealing with weightier themes and incomparable as cinema, *The Killer,* in plot, structure, and violence, functions as a modern kung-fu movie, with pistols substituted for fists. Every bullet equals a punch, which produces a correspondingly higher body count. As with many Hong Kong films, the dubbing, whether in Cantonese or English, is terrible. The English-subtitled version is far more enjoyable.

The trademarks of Woo's singular cinema include constant, narrative camera movement, an emotional atmosphere in which every exchange—however profound or meaningless—is played at maximum intensity, and an overriding sentimentality that at first seems deranged. There's also a strange homoeroticism between Yun-Fat and the cop; in Woo films no relationship is so important as trust between man and man. Woo's women are either ornamental or so stylized as to exist only as metaphors. The nightclub singer is both.

With so much blood on his hands, Yun-Fat's hit man must atone, and so he does, as only a Woo hero can: by spilling even more blood. The final action sequence, an endless, cathartic shoot-out in an empty church, more than makes up for the tedious, religiously weird, expository passages that lead up to it. A hundred men croak in this final blow-out, which is filled with loving camera-caresses of machine guns and doves soaring to the ceiling. Images sacred and profane swirl together as men die and die, with each death choreographed for maximum screen impact.

Cinema does not get any wackier or more compelling. The gunfights go on and on, and every minute is more imaginative, irresistible, exciting, and beautiful than the last. Woo is the ultimate poet of on-screen violence: Everything else in his pictures is secondary.

Other recommended rentals directed by John Woo:
A Better Tomorrow
Bullet in the Head
Hard-Boiled (see page 55)
Hard Target

Kind Hearts and Coronets

Impeccably British irony :**ATTITUDE**
Civilized deadpan comedy :**MOOD**

DIRECTOR: Robert Hamer (1949—U.K.)
CAST: Alec Guinness, Dennis Price, Valerie Hobson, Joan Greenwood
IN ENGLISH; B/W

Dennis Price and Joan Greenwood in *Kind Hearts and Coronets*

A film of painstakingly good manners and appallingly bad taste, as our hero relies upon only the most polite murders and adultery to advance himself up the social ladder to the exalted place he feels he deserves.

Thwarted by his Edwardian-era family's refusal to recognize him as a rightful member (due to his bastardy), Dennis Price finds himself cut out of the inheritance and title he craves. His well-bred British method of righting this egregious wrong? Simple. He vows to kill every member of the offending family who stands between him and the title. There are, after all, only nine of them.

Being an inventive, engaging, and hardworking young chap, Price employs a variety of methods to dispatch his victims: poison, explosives, falls from high places . . . As he murders, Price also deals with the affections of two very different women: the now-married sweetheart of his innocent youth, the essence of bald-faced conniving as played by Joan Greenwood; and the widow of one of his victims, a study in regal repression as embodied by Valerie Hobson. Greenwood offers him solace for her earlier snubs; Hobson offers him the upper-class companion he always desired. Alas, one is hot but unworthy, the other perfectly suitable but lamentably frigid. What's a confused young murderer to do? Why, take satisfaction from both at once, lying all the while.

The family members whom Price murders bear a disconcerting resemblance to one another, and for good reason. From the sepulchral bank president to the alcoholic photographer to the pontifical bishop to the meddling old maid of an aunt, every one is portrayed by Alec Guinness. Alec shifts his walk, his accent, and his manner, and seems to recede further into each character as the film proceeds. His absolute absence of actorly vanity is a wonder to behold. Price, who bears a disconcerting resemblance to Guinness himself, holds his own in the many scenes he shares with the master, and grants Guinness all the room he needs to shape his characters. Their deft, knowing interplay forms the core of the film.

Never a voice is raised, never an act of violence shown, and always in the background comes the carefully modulated tones of our homicidal narrator. His paradoxical calm in the midst of carnage only makes his claims to civilization (the English upper class from which he was hurled) all the more cynical. And the film makes no pretense of condemning Price for either his crimes or his ambition. It presents Edwardian society as well worth obliterating and the upper classes as a worthy, though corrupt and corrupting, goal. Our hero never demonstrates the slightest remorse, as befits a gentlemen of the old school.

An adult exercise in irony, crafted to perfection, presented in a flowing, unhurried rhythm. An unmistakable product of its age: the ultimate—and funniest—British black comedy.

The King of Comedy

Showbiz with the gloves off :**ATTITUDE**
Neurotic, nerve-wracking comedy :**MOOD**

DIRECTOR: Martin Scorsese (1982—U.S.A.)
CAST: Robert De Niro, Jerry Lewis, Sandra Bernhard, Ed Herlihy
IN ENGLISH; COLOR

Jerry Lewis and Robert De Niro in *The King of Comedy*

Pure obsessive vitriol; the most accurate statement made on the success processes of American showbiz and on the showbiz state of American consciousness. American showbiz is a vicious business, but
everyone wants to be a star, regardless of talent, worth, or ability.

Rupert Pupkin—Robert De Niro in a role of toweringly repellent
creepiness—is no exception. Pupkin is a fiendish characterization.
He hates himself and desires public acclaim with equal avidity. He
deems himself a stand-up comic but never performs in public. Among
the losers who congregate for autographs outside any opening in New
York, Rupert is the most strident, the most vigilant, the most ready
to castigate any star who won't stop and be nice. To cap off Rupert's
empty life, he has an obsession: Jerry Langford, the king of talk TV.

Jerry Lewis, acting with an unprecedented controlled fury, plays
Langford, a filmic version of Johnny Carson. Rupert wants to be on
Jerry's show. In fact, Rupert *wants* Jerry's show. After being brushed
off repeatedly, and always in the most humiliating fashion, Rupert
snaps. With the aid of Sandra Bernhard—exuding a pre-fame and totally uncut version of her uniquely menacing sexuality—he kidnaps
Jerry. The only acceptable ransom: an opening monologue on Jerry's
show.

Martin Scorsese is the master of discomfort, and plucks the reins of unease as expertly as Hitchcock manipulated for suspense. In the manner of Godard's *Weekend,* Scorsese takes our suppressed aggression, self-interest, vanity, and greed, and turns up the volume. Pupkin wears on the outside what most conceal deep within. A bizarre anomaly when the film was released, Pupkin now seems the very model of 90's goal-oriented behavior.

Scorsese provides no easy answers: Pupkin is an unbearable loser, a galling, willfully unsocialized geek who refuses to understand how the world works. Yet those who reject him are so needlessly unkind that even Pupkin becomes an object of sympathy. And in the end, Jerry was right to fear him. Pupkin fools everyone; his secret weapon is that he can take more abuse than his enemies can dish out. To succeed in American showbiz, Scorsese suggests, that may be the only talent required.

After decades of pretending it didn't exist, Jerry Lewis finally unveils his formidable dark side. He gives a remarkably ego-free performance. Lewis's interplay with De Niro is funny in a sinister way, and deeply unnerving. The supporting actors are terrific: Shelley Hack shines as an unpleasant talent coordinator trying to make Pupkin understand her polite rejections. And, no one moves a camera or reveals obsession like Scorsese.

Certainly not a morality tale, the story lies between drama and comedy. By turns it's funny, unsettling, surreal, and unbearable. Consider it an exercise in truth through exaggeration. Rent this and *Sweet Smell of Success* (see page 165) and all your questions about showbiz will be answered.

Other recommended rentals directed by Martin Scorsese:
The Color of Money
GoodFellas
Mean Streets
Raging Bull
Taxi Driver

The Lady Eve

Sophisticated screwball :**ATTITUDE**
Amusing madcap comedy :**MOOD**

DIRECTOR: Preston Sturges (1941—U.S.A.)
CAST: Henry Fonda, Barbara Stanwyck, William Demarest, Charles
   Coburn
IN ENGLISH; B/W

Charles Coburn, Barbara Stanwyck, William Demarest, and Henry Fonda in
The Lady Eve

The smartest of all screwball comedies, with dialogue that flows so
smoothly you may not notice the best lines until after the movie's over.

Less frantic than *The Miracle of Morgan's Creek* (see page 104), more
seamless and controlled than *Sullivan's Travels,* and displaying a genuine sweetness that Sturges seldom voiced overtly, *The Lady Eve* is the
least insulting screwball comedy, and the most touching.

Henry Fonda has been "up the Amazon" for a year, researching
snakes. "You know me," he says. "Nothing but reptiles." On an ocean
liner headed for home, Barbara Stanwyck spots him as a potential
sucker. She and her dad (Charles Coburn in a relaxed, avuncular turn)

are a pair of hustlers whose motto is: "Let us be crooked but never common." They intend to fleece Fonda at cards but Stanwyck falls in love with him for real. Before she can confess her profession, Fonda learns the truth and, heartbroken but outraged, dumps her. She vows revenge.

Impersonating an English lady, she shows up at Fonda's parents' estate. Convinced that she's a new person—a look-alike of his lost sweetheart—Fonda is delighted at the idea of finding his forbidden love in a socially acceptable form. He pursues Stanwyck with all his clumsy might. William Demarest, playing Fonda's bodyguard and guardian angel, thinks she's the same old hustle and sets out to prove it. Fonda and Stanwyck dance around all obstacles, playing games and exchanging barbs until both open their hearts.

Fonda was never so relaxed, so simultaneously daft and dignified. The physical prowess of his pratfalls might surprise you. He proves his versatility, delivering an a amiable guilelessness laid over a resolutely independent core. His role is primarily reactive, but he's a perfect straight man. Stanwyck floats through the story, glamorous and regal. She connects to her tough side with ease and delivers Sturges's cobra-quick repartee with a knowing wit. The actors in Sturges's films often seem to revel in their performances; maybe it's the thrill of speaking such inventive dialogue. Fonda and Stanwyck are no exception. They appear happy in their work.

Unlike *Miracle,* which runs on adrenaline and inventiveness, *Lady* is relaxed enough to appear occasionally dated. The opening forty-five minutes rush by nonstop, one gag, one plot motivation, one wrinkle after another. After such dizzying virtuosity, it's only natural that Sturges take a break, and he does, for a ten-minute transition sequence that sets up the second half of the picture. During that transition, he reverts to a string of dated time-killing gags, shot with less than his usual imagination. If you find yourself tuning out, be patient. . . .

Sturges's camera is unusually quiet, the better to focus on the brilliant dialogue. Fonda and Stanwyck, held in Sturges's typically endless two-shot close-ups, chat amiably on, nailing every nuance of every complex line. As always, the excellence of the production—the costumes, lighting, the playing of the lesser characters, the large-scale gags, and the small-scale quips—never calls attention to itself, but is woven into Sturges's palpable joy at making movies.

Other recommended rentals directed by Preston Sturges:
The Great McGinty
The Miracle of Morgan's Creek (see page 104)
Sullivan's Travels

The Last Movie

Glorious mess **:ATTITUDE**
Wild-ass Hollywood art movie **:MOOD**

DIRECTOR: Dennis Hopper (1971—U.S.A.)
CAST: Dennis Hopper, Kris Kristofferson, Don Gordon, Stella Garcia
IN ENGLISH; COLOR

This is Dennis Hopper's fucked-up magnum opus, his Great American Movie, the picture that was to certify his anointment as God of New Young Hollywood, that would cement his reputation as America's answer to all the arty Europeans. Unfortunately, what it cemented was his reputation as an egomaniac who would ruin any project with his demented schemes, short attention span, and inhuman drug and alcohol consumption. Now that Hopper's genius is widely recognized—he's so revered he gets to direct commercial tripe—it may be hard to remember just how far he fell, and why.

Easy Rider, which Hopper directed, cost three hundred thousand dollars and grossed a hundred million. The studios gave Hopper carte blanche and he went off to South America with his pals (Don Gordon, Kris Kristofferson, Peter Fonda, Sylvia Miles, Dean Stockwell), his idols (Henry Fonda and director Sam Fuller), and a crew. There he pissed away incalculable amounts of money, prestige, and credibility, shooting with no discernible script or purpose. Or so said the businessmen back home.

After months of budget overruns and arguments over editing, the studio seized Hopper's film and refused to release it. The conflict was legendary, and until recently the arguments could never be settled, because no one ever saw the thing. Thanks to videotape, though, it's clear that Hopper was on the track of something miraculous but for whatever reasons lacked the courage of his convictions while editing the final third of the film. Or that as a (totally self-destructive) director he preferred anarchy to a more conventionally satisfying conclusion. Perhaps it's a combination of the two.

For all its tortured narrative, there is a plot, at least until the final thirty minutes. Hopper plays "Kansas," a stuntman on a western being shot in the Peruvian Andes (and what a western, with Henry and Peter Fonda, directed by Sam Fuller). The shoot ends but Kansas stays behind, fascinated with his whore girlfriend and a strange ritual being played out on the abandoned movie set. The Peruvian Indians construct mock cameras, lights, and sound machines out of bamboo and are shooting their own movie. Trouble is, the Indians confuse the make-believe of filming with reality and their movie violence is real; in their shoot-outs, people get shot. And, unlike Hopper, the Indians have a script. At the climax of their filming, they intend to sacrifice Kansas to the god of the camera.

Hopper interjects several jokey/arty references to the fact that he's making a film throughout the film; they're irritating. But he cheats us out of the considerable suspense built around the question of Kansas's fate by supplying several different endings in succession. He also tries to remind us that Kansas can't really die, because he's only a character in a movie—at best, a puerile notion; at worst, infuriating.

The film is shot with a raw beauty, and acted as if everyone's lives hung in the balance. Hopper, Gordon, and Fuller are particularly fine. The scenery, which Hopper treats as irrelevant background to the higher drama of filming (exactly how a film crew on location would perceive it), is breathtaking. The western within the film features some of the most dynamic and enthralling camera movement to ever be used in a real western. It's so much fun!

Hopper tried to merge a personal statement, a comment-on-cinema art movie, with a big-budget Hollywood action flick. His failure is infinitely more interesting than the successes of a thousand commercial hacks.

It's a stunning monument to artistic courage and artistic confusion, a truly funny picture, a wide-open window to the young Hollywood of the early 1970s in all its glorious excess—and a lot more entertaining than its reputation might lead you to believe.

Other recommended rentals directed by Dennis Hopper:
Colors
Easy Rider
Out of the Blue (see page 115)

Le Dernier Combat (aka The Last Battle)

French sci-fi **:ATTITUDE**
Offbeat silent epic **:MOOD**

DIRECTOR: Luc Besson (1984—France)
CAST: Jean Reno, Maurice Lamy, Pierre Jolivet
NO DIALOGUE; B/W

If it sounds like a parody of the worst possible filmic idea—silent French science fiction—then think of it instead as director Luc Besson's (*La Femme Nikita, Subway, The Professional*) screen debut. He wrote and directed this low-budget wonder, which, in its physical and emotional evocation of a fully realized and believable future can only be compared to George Lucas's *THX 1138*. Where George spent his limited money on sets, special effects, and costumes, Besson spends his on atmosphere and camera movement. Besson's vision is more languid and his film more of a contemplation, but he builds suspense and dread far more ably than Lucas.

The tale follows a lonely survivor as he moves through the desolate wasteland of a postapocalyptic urban center. His character never speaks and has no name. He lives alone in a dilapidated apartment building and ceaselessly scours the ruined cityscape for food, tools, and weapons. An appalling beastlike giant—a brutal battering ram of a man—serves as our hero's nemesis. They make war on one another's apartment/fortresses, dueling to invent the most crudely ingenious devices of war. These grisly tools are triumphs of Besson's witty, gear-oriented, and violent imagination. Rube Goldberg has *rien* on Luc Besson.

Very French, *n'est-ce pas*? A formerly sophisticated culture has been reduced to two savages. The savage who most cleverly recycles the garbage of his culture's former heyday will kill the other and triumph in their empty world. Only in the climactic final shot do we learn of the higher purpose behind their apparently pointless and nonstop struggle.

Our hero plays every situation, however grave or amusing, in stone-faced silence. He has a wonderful physical presence, a powerful gravity, and his clownlike features wear a mask of tragedy. No American actor could convey the same impression of mingled profundity and barbarism, especially considering that he hasn't a word of dialogue. To call the film "silent" is inaccurate, though. Besson fills the sound track with creaks, gunshots, engines, wind, doors, and footsteps. Our hero never speaks because there is no one for him to speak to.

"Silent" might also suggest tedious, which this is not. It's Luc Besson, which means a combination of action- and art-film conventions. Every scene features an inventive camera move, edit, or really wacky action on the part of our hero. Commitment to shooting dialogue-free means commitment to mood and atmosphere; few first features show such eccentric personality or expert narrative thrills. (Most first-time directors concentrate on one or the other.) For all the arty Frenchness on display in his later features, Besson loves thrillers above all. He never subsumes the thrills of this story to any pretentious film concept. In fact, the filming is designed to support the whammies, and boy, does it.

And, as quest epics go, it's the perfect length: less than ninety minutes. Besson knew that no matter how inventive he might be, no audience would watch a movie without dialogue for more than an hour and a half.

Weird, funny, hypnotic, and irresistible. The first hint of Besson's unique merging of American mayhem and French art film.

Other recommended rentals directed by Luc Besson:

The Big Blue

La Femme Nikita

Subway (subtitled version only; beware the dubbed version)

Let It Ride

Endearing verbal slapstick :ATTITUDE
Good-hearted, gag-filled, intelligent comedy :MOOD

DIRECTOR: Joe Pytka (1989—U.S.A.)
CAST: Richard Dreyfuss, Teri Garr, David Johansen, Michelle Phillips
IN ENGLISH; COLOR

Such a lovable, lightweight, class-act comedy, that its absence of wide success qualifies as a genuine tragedy. A rare find: a contemporary film to make adults laugh without ever feeling insulted, patronized, or that they have to chase the kids out of the room. Backing up the humor is a genuine romantic sweetness that makes this a perfect date movie.

Richard Dreyfuss plays a down-on-his-luck horse player who, for once, is "having a very good day." His good day runs the gamut of picking serial winners, several sexual propositions, conversations with horses, and a reunion with his wife. In the tradition of track movies, the back-story is packed with a collection of supporting characters usually described as "Runyonesque," which here means they speak their own colorful made-up slang.

Teri Garr plays Dreyfuss's long-suffering wife, rubber-faced David Johansen plays Dreyfuss's best buddy, and Jennifer Tilly (from Woody Allen's *Bullets Over Broadway*) is hilarious as a moll with a heart of gold and a voice to melt lead.

Pytka is perhaps the most famous and best paid of all directors who specialize in commercials. This is his feature debut. Perhaps he tries too hard, perhaps he's not quite suited to full-length filmmaking. But if certain scenes are overdone, Pytka errs only from an excess of devotion to what he knows best—gags.

Pytka strays into old habits: several scenes are lit like "Miller Time," and some jokes are needlessly broad, as if Pytka forgets that our attention span can be longer than thirty seconds. Even so, Pytka's timing, editing, and use of character actors suggests genuine comic brilliance. As does the wry, contained performance of Richard Dreyfuss. He's never been so low key or so likable. The dramatic space he grants, scene by scene, to actors whom he could blow off the screen anytime he wanted, is a paradigm of genuine collaborative generosity. Dreyfuss even avoids his arrogant, chin-in-the-air barking style of speech that can be so irritating.

The finale so perfectly treads a tightrope between cornball and redemption that you'll laugh as you cry without ever feeling manipulated. Pytka, and Dreyfuss's charm and remarkable absence of cynicism, make *Let It Ride* not only a great date movie—love lost, temptation, the intervention of good luck, love found once more—but also a great comedy.

Lolita

Forbidden love **:ATTITUDE**
Slow, perverse comedy/tragedy **:MOOD**

DIRECTOR: Stanley Kubrick (1961—U.K.)
CAST: Peter Sellers, James Mason, Shelley Winters, Sue Lyons
IN ENGLISH; B/W

Sue Lyons as Lolita

It's an ironic combination: the most controlling and controlled director in film adapting the classic novel of impulse and obsession. . . .
While less explicit than the novel, Kubrick's adaptation is remarkably
nuanced and attuned to Nabokov's intentions. Kubrick's ironic distance serves him well; he may have less compassion for the characters
than Nabokov, but he understands how they should translate to the
screen.

Humbert Humbert, a gentleman of letters—James Mason at his
most fey and repressed—becomes obsessed with Lolita, the teenage
daughter of an American widow—Shelley Winters in the role she
played a thousand times thereafter: the oversexed, grasping domina-
trix. Humbert marries Winters to be near Lolita and, when she dies,
runs away with the girl. Once alone with his object of adoration,
Humbert's dream deteriorates; Lolita is too American and teenaged
to be commanded, sinister forces pursue them, and the girl abandons
Humbert.

Though Humbert's obsession with Lolita is rendered in amusing
and sick detail—made clear in the opening credits as Humbert
paints Lolita's toenails—Kubrick shifts the emphasis so that an all-
pervading tone of perversity rules. The font of that tone is Peter Sellers, presenting an impersonation of an American neurotic unequaled
in screen history for detail, range, quick-wittedness, or self-loathing.

Forgotten in discussions over Kubrick's pitiless disapproval of
Humbert is the awe-inspiring genius of Peter Sellers's shape-shifting
immersion into the psychotic character of Quilty. Quilty pursues
Lolita out of lust and Humbert out of sadism. In creating this hipster
madman of a thousand masks, Sellers proves himself excruciatingly
hip. If you think Robin Williams reveals borderline psychosis when
he improvises, check out Sellers.

Kubrick said: "Truthful and valid ideas are so multifaceted that
they do not yield themselves to frontal assault." Accordingly, he explains little, preferring to capture the action in a cultivated, unadorned
style. Everyone's neurotic in this world, and Kubrick leaves it up to us
to determine the truth lurking in the subtext. The usual Kubrickian
themes emerge nonetheless: emotional obsession is degrading, and
man's folly is the most reliable source of humor and pathos in this life.
Poor, tormented, ridiculous Humbert. . . . Kubrick cuts him no slack.
Quilty seems admirable by comparison because Quilty, though evil,

freely admits his perversity. Kubrick doesn't seem to mind Humbert's lust for little girls; it's Humbert's hypocritical claims to piety that make him a villain.

Kubrick's meticulous construction serves the story well. He surrenders his usual narrative methods and accepts the form of the book as the form of the film. As a result, this picture shifts moods and locations chapter by chapter; perhaps contributing to its slow pace. It's a lovely film, shot in low-contrast grays, with the least intrusive, most subtle camera work of any Kubrick picture.

Not a day at the beach, though: a serious, cruelly funny, slow British art movie of a Russian novel about the core of the American Experience. Sometimes grim, always insightful, and, despite the mean-spirited humor, singularly moving.

Other recommended rentals directed by Stanley Kubrick:

2001: A Space Odyssey
Barry Lyndon (see page 10)
A Clockwork Orange
Dr. Strangelove or: How I Learned to Stop Worrying and Love the Bomb
Full Metal Jacket
The Killing
Paths of Glory (see page 125)

The Long Goodbye

Hollywood as moral universe :**ATTITUDE**
Cynical, ironic private-eye suspense :**MOOD**

DIRECTOR: Robert Altman (1972—U.S.A.)
CAST: Elliot Gould, Henry Gibson, Sterling Hayden, Jim Bouton
IN ENGLISH; COLOR

A modernist, absurd take on the classic Raymond Chandler novel featuring Hollywood private detective Philip Marlowe. Elliot Gould brings an offhand, shambling grace to a character burned into America's memory (by Humphrey Bogart) as hard-boiled and in control.

Gould's Marlowe never even attempts control: He's much too aware of the power of fate.

For Altman, Marlowe remains a man of the 1940s trapped in the 1970s. Marlowe wears old suits, drives an antique car, and holds himself to an outdated moral code. His morality includes loyalty, fair play, and a lack of greed. Any man adhering to such a code, Altman contends, will experience serious problems living and working in modern Los Angeles.

Alienated yet determined to survive, Marlowe's mantra is "It's okay with me," by which he keeps himself separate from the grasping of those around him. Marlowe's personality is both his salvation and the root cause of his lack of success—the struggle between the two (personal morality versus career-striving) is a recurring Altman theme.

More than pace or rhythm, Altman is a master of mood, and his sequence shifts usually depend on one mood ending and another taking hold. This narrative shift in mood is enhanced by Leigh Brackett's sarcastic but sincere screenplay. (Brackett contributed to the screenplay of another Raymond Chandler work, 1946's classic, *The Big Sleep.*) Brackett sees Marlowe and Hollywood through the prism of thirty years of personal experience; her nasty humor and its brutal violence give the story an incisive edge.

The constantly shifting, constantly searching camera mirrors Marlowe's quest, and reveals a shadowy world hidden beneath L.A.'s sunshine. That world includes a drunken author, his scheming wife, and a vicious, neurotic gangster played by director Mark Rydell (*Cinderella Liberty*). Everyone except Marlowe is neurotic in that L.A. showbiz way: They're neurotic and proud of it.

Sterling Hayden, almost unrecognizable behind a huge hippie beard and gray tangled mane, is the doomed writer. *Ball Four* author Jim Bouton plays Marlowe's missing friend. Short-time 1970s celebrity—and erotic powerhouse—Nina Van Palant is the femme fatale, and Arnold Schwarzenegger enjoys his screen debut as a hoodlum tough guy. Blink, and you might miss him.

A hundred wonderful, hidden jokes (and references to other films noir) run through the film. Among the most subversive is that the film's theme song plays on whatever music source is nearest. Gould listens to a jazz version of the song on his car radio; when he walks from his car into a supermarket, the Hollywood Strings' Muzak rendition plays in the store. When Marlowe visits a remote Mexican village, the funeral band marches by blaring the theme.

A touching, funny, suspenseful parody of detective movies that may be the best detective movie ever made.

Other recommended rentals directed by Robert Altman:
Brewster McCloud
Buffalo Bill & the Indians
McCabe & Mrs. Miller (see page 102)
The Player

Macbeth

Shakespeare as nightmare **:ATTITUDE**
Blood-drenched, action-packed classic **:MOOD**

DIRECTOR: Roman Polanski (1971—U.K./U.S.A.)
CAST: Jon Finch, Francesca Annis, Martin Shaw
IN ENGLISH; COLOR

Where Laurence Olivier (see *Henry V,* page 59) is overly formal and Kenneth Branagh (*Henry V, Much Ado About Nothing*) deliberately downmarket, Polanski approaches the Bard seeking only the truth. And for Polanski—making his first film since the murder of his wife Sharon Tate at the hands of Charles Manson's minions—truth equals doom, soaked twice over in blood and guilt. Polanski's grief guides him effortlessly to the most nightmarish aspects of the play. He ritualizes the horror, shooting the murders, sword-fights, and witches' rituals with a gleeful energy and inventiveness reminiscent of *The Adventures of Robin Hood* (see page 1).

From the opening sequence—which begins with the horrible witches on a barren shore and ends with a warrior hacking open the back of a wounded opponent—Polanski establishes the tone. No heroism, no salvation, only mayhem, and lots of it. It's a primitive world and Polanski, eschewing his usual ironic approach, gets down and dirty. The virtue of his technique is a Shakespeare with something for everyone: superb acting for the cognoscenti, and swell sword-fights for the less informed.

Polanski's gift to this genre is to take the Royal Shakespeare Company out of their cloistered sets and into the damp, dirty, and foreboding Welsh countryside. His revolutionary use of handheld cameras frees his actors from the constipated Englishness of their training, and the result is Shakespeare as you've never heard it. That is, Shakespeare as normal human conversation. Every other Shakespeare film director sublimates all to the words, but Polanski prefers that the speeches serve the action. Surprisingly, his approach proves the most moving. It might not work for other Shakespeare, but for *Macbeth* it's a daring and powerful stroke.

Jon Finch, as Macbeth, finds a speaking rhythm that deformalizes his soliloquies. A vocal delivery without melodrama means less poetry, but it engenders a better understanding and more forward plot movement. Finch's voice could fill a cathedral; his reticent, inward-turning performance leads us straight to Macbeth's dark heart. Finch's Macbeth may not be the most charismatic dude in the world, but Martin Shaw's tender "Banquo" and Terence Baylor's rough-and-ready "Macduff" more than make up for him.

The expository moments, and those featuring Francesca Annis as Lady Macbeth, drift. Polanski demonstrates little interest in the interior struggles of women. Polanski's obsession is the murderous impulse in men. His may be a harsh, reductive reading of the play, but it's neither inaccurate nor inappropriate. Whatever its shortcomings, this is the most direct, heartfelt Shakespeare on the screen. And, by shaving off what doesn't intrigue him, Polanski ends up with Macbeth on a rocket sled—the story races by.

The film, like the play, is not for the squeamish. Polanski exorcises his nightmares by making them ours, with all the gory detail such a perverse mission requires. Plus, unlikely as it may sound, brief, illuminating moments of loveliness, humor, and humanity, with more compassion for all concerned—including poor Macbeth—than you might think possible.

Other recommended rentals directed by Roman Polanski:

Chinatown

Knife in the Water

Repulsion

The Tenant

Mad Dog and Glory

Geek love :**ATTITUDE**
Quirky cop movie/love story :**MOOD**

DIRECTOR: John McNaughton (1993—U.S.A.)
CAST: Robert De Niro, Bill Murray, Uma Thurman, David Caruso,
      Kathy Baker
IN ENGLISH; COLOR

A whimsical, violent mixture of love story, crime story, and comedy, with a plot that might at first sound like a low-budget independent, until you hear the list of heavyweights involved.

Author Richard Price (*Clockers*) wrote the screenplay; Wim Wenders's cameraman, Robbie Müller, served as cinematographer; Martin Scorsese produced, and the cast includes Bill Murray, Robert De Niro, Uma Thurman, Kathy Baker, and David Caruso in the role that served as the prototype for his character on *NYPD Blue*. This is a class act: top-of-the-line professionals devoting themselves to a picture they knew hadn't a prayer of commercial success.

De Niro is Mad Dog, a Chicago cop, a lonely nerd who dislikes violence and will do anything to avoid a confrontation. By interrupting a robbery, De Niro saves the life of Frank Milo (Bill Murray), a vicious Chicago gangster with pretensions to stand-up comedy. Frank gives Mad Dog a thank-you present in the form of Uma Thurman. She owes Frank and will do anything Mad Dog wants for one week.

Uma comes through Mad Dog's door as a whore, but she goes out a princess. De Niro perceives in her sterling qualities she may or may not possess and, having fallen for her, refuses to let her go. Frank demands she be returned. Mad Dog stands up for himself and a showdown is inevitable.

Frank Milo is obviously a madman, and Murray brings all his psychoses to the fore. Frank's good at being a mobster but suffers from being smarter than everyone else in his mobster's universe. He sees a possible new friend in De Niro, but underestimates Mad Dog's purity of character. Mad Dog—a preposterously straight arrow—lies, cheats, and steals to keep Thurman; love is making a man out of him. Frank, ruthless and prone to violent solutions, isn't interested in Mad Dog's inner journey; he wants his girl back.

De Niro plays Mad Dog as a man slowly coming out of his shell. In a protracted love scene with Uma—played in dead silence—Mad Dog rediscovers the joys of sex, companionship, and of life itself. To see the nerd's self-loathing wiped off his face and replaced by the faintest belief in the possibility of happiness might just make you cry. While Bill Murray performs with his usual smirk to the audience, De Niro totally invests his character in a low-key and little-known performance.

As the story races along, the pleasures of the film reveal themselves: Mad Dog's struggle to become whole, Bill Murray's knowing stare, David Caruso's air of menace, and screenwriter Richard Price's understanding of the self-promoting mythmaking that both cops and criminals enjoy.

No picture this idiosyncratic comes free of dead spots or foolish moments, but they're overshadowed by the force, commitment, and humor of the performances. Watch attentively and the mood will take hold from the opening shot.

Other recommended rentals directed by John McNaughton:
Henry: Portrait of a Serial Killer
Normal Life

Man of Flowers

Perverse sweetness **:ATTITUDE**
Kinky art movie/comedy **:MOOD**

DIRECTOR: Paul Cox (1983—Australia)
CAST: Alyson Best, Norman Kaye, Chris Haywood
IN ENGLISH; COLOR

A winning, offbeat exploration of the difficulty of maintaining innocence, the lure of fantasy, and the life-shaping power of erotic desire. Taking a semi-Freudian, semi-fantasist approach, Australian director Paul Cox creates a strange little romance.

So antimacho—but resolutely heterosexual—as to provide commentary not only on Australian notions of manhood, but also on Australian cinema, *Man* features no chase scenes, no violence, no overt sex, and several lovely nude scenes. Is it a funny art film, or an arty comedy?

Neither. It's a Paul Cox movie, which means a mix of humor, insight, strange pacing, quirky characters, and a palpable belief in cosmic destiny: In a Paul Cox film, everyone gets what they deserve. Think of him as the Tom Robbins of Australian Cinema—and like Robbins his main interests are men and women together, and how a pacifist man might enforce his will on a violent world.

The mortician-faced Norman Kaye plays an easily exploited, slightly mad recluse made recently wealthy by a large inheritance. A man at home with art and inanimate beauty, he's prey to the sharks of the real world. Among these is the coke-snorting, artist-wannabe boyfriend of Alyson Best. Best plays a kindhearted artist's model who strips, in the most chaste way, for Norman every Wednesday to the sounds of Donizetti's *Lucia di Lammermoor*.

Watching Alyson undress excites Norman, and his arousal fills him with shame. The core of the film is Norman's search for self-worth and companionship through exploring his erotic side, and Alyson's search for the same via her attempts to escape her boyfriend. When their quests unite, Norman proves himself more capable than he appears. That he slowly comes to accept his own sexual desires is presented by Cox as a quiet triumph.

Cox's pace is relaxed, his sense of humor extremely dry (Norman's hapless psychiatrist complains to Norman about premature ejaculation—"I watched other men make love to my wife until I got the hang of it," he says), and his outlook benign. Norman proves a complicated character; Cox teaches us about his upbringing via flashback, during which we meet Norman's overly expressive mother and his stern, withholding father, played by none other than director Werner Herzog (*Aguirre, the Wrath of God*; see page 3). Herzog, a fearsome father figure to many arty directors, portrays the essence of stiff-necked paternal disapproval.

Cox's hero is as delicate as the flowers he loves, but his delicacy is wound around a core of steel-hard integrity. And in the end, it's the gentle champion who—much to his own surprise—earns the love of the worthy maiden(s).

Truly strange, but never inaccessible or dull. Through the vehicle of an endearing, if unlikely, date movie, Cox explores repression, lust, destructive relationships, self-loathing, self-acceptance, and redemption. Weird and wonderful.

Other recommended rentals directed by Paul Cox:
Lonely Hearts
Vincent: The Life and Death of Vincent van Gogh

The Man Who Would Be King

A grand old time :**ATTITUDE**
Epic adventure of the old school :**MOOD**

DIRECTOR: John Huston (1975—U.S.A.)
CAST: Michael Caine, Sean Connery, Shakira Caine
IN ENGLISH; COLOR

Sean Connery and Michael Caine in *The Man Who Would Be King*

In the time of Rudyard Kipling (in a tale based on his short story) two English ex-soldiers—Sean Connery and Michael Caine—travel to a far-off land beyond the Himalayas. They cross snowy mountains and plains, they ford mighty rivers. When they reach this mythological country, they train a modern army of natives. Their goal is nothing less than national conquest; they want to rule their own kingdom. In the midst of a battle, one of the Englishmen is mistaken for the legendary long-lost son of Alexander the Great and declared a deity. The two friends rule as king and king's advisor, until the king starts to believe in his own tomfoolery. He behaves as if he really were divine, and the roof caves in. As all colonial adventurers must, the boys learn that there's no justice like primitive justice and no sin like hubris.

To his advantage, John Huston (*The Asphalt Jungle, Treasure of the Sierra Madre*) was not young when he directed this rollicking, offhand ode to/satire of imperialism. The years seem to have made Huston less cynical, more willing to laugh at man's folly while documenting its inescapable pull. Huston clearly loves the epic stuff. Though he stages battles like Cecil B. DeMille—with hordes of native extras, and all shot on remote locations—Huston undercuts the serious moments with farce and makes certain that the humorous moments are profound. The maturity of Huston's vision, and Connery's and Caine's willingness to makes fools of themselves, combine to produce a larger-than-life atmosphere that makes the film a true adventure.

Connery brings a genial stupidity to his character, playing a more or less straightforward oaf who is amazed at his elevation to royalty and determined to do the thing properly. Caine plays a more conniving sort, a man who sees all the angles but cannot steer Connery away from disaster.

Everyone appears to be having a ball. Connery has seldom been more exuberant or endearing. He moves like a shaggy dog, trying to be dignified and looking all the more ridiculous as a result. The story, the players, and the script possess a natural exuberance that the Indiana Jones pictures strive for but cannot attain. Think of the swaggering, piratical fun of H. Rider Haggard's novel (and movie) *King Solomon's Mine*—white men with delusions of grandeur having grand adventures until the force of native culture proves too much for them.

Naturally, given Huston's age and his notion of things, there are some remarkably cheesy transitions, several unfortunate (Kiplingesque) jokes based on the poor understanding of English by Indians, and locker-room gags about men and women, all designed to amuse the average eighth-grader. Whether they're included because Huston likes them or because he's playing to a certain market, who can say?

An old-fashioned, big-scale adventure, acted with love and cunning, directed with skill and forbearance. Another perfect rental: a family movie, a date movie, a picture that seems like pure fun to kids but carries concealed depth and hidden humor for adults. Fine battles, sweeping vistas, grand locations—and Sean Connery.

Other recommended rentals directed by John Huston:

The Asphalt Jungle
Fat City
The Red Badge of Courage
Treasure of the Sierra Madre

McCabe & Mrs. Miller

Art western **:ATTITUDE**
Lyrical showdown/romance **:MOOD**

DIRECTOR: Robert Altman (1971–U.S.A.)
CAST: Warren Beatty, Julie Christie, Michael Murphy, William Devane
IN ENGLISH; COLOR

Warren Beatty and Julie Christie in *McCabe & Mrs. Miller*

Where Peckinpah used a sledgehammer (*The Wild Bunch*) to dismantle the western, Altman wields a scalpel. When he's done, the old myths—heroism, selfless community, redemptive love—are dead. In their place is a new mythology, composed of Altman's modern themes: the destructive absurdity of existence, the impossibility of emotional connection, the assured triumph of futility, and man's obliviousness to his own fatal flaws.

Warren Beatty plays McCabe, a small-time roaming gambler who stumbles into a backwater mining town. McCabe tries to build the town into his own small empire, but proves too much an amateur to battle the better-funded and more violent empire-builders who rule the West.

McCabe's tiny holdings include "the finest whorehouse in the territory," managed by Julie Christie as Mrs. Miller. McCabe is supposed to be her boss, but she's too tough for him. The interaction between Beatty and Christie (lovers at the time) is magical. McCabe falls hard for Mrs. Miller—she brings out the sentimentality Altman finds lurking in every American man of violence—but Mrs. Miller prefers opium to love. Thus, Altman reinvents the western to present his favorite thwarters of man's will: failed romantic love and big business.

There are no heroes in Altman's West, only degrees of cowardice. Those who play fair are weak, and the strong shoot the weak in the back. Altman's art transcends his message, however. *McCabe,* for all its tragedy, is never depressing. Altman's grace and daring, Beatty's gently self-mocking performance, and the gripping, if rather traditionally told story frames the western in a whole new way.

Using improvised and overlapping dialogue, Altman's characters describe themselves unknowingly. What they say reveals the disparity between what they believe their place in the world to be and what everybody else knows it is. Here, more of Altman's favorites themes: how power relationships determine the nature of society, and how ultimately all power struggles must eventually be resolved through violence—physical, economic, or emotional. McCabe faces each with varying levels of skill.

McCabe's misfortune is that he tries to be a lover when he should be a fighter, he thinks when he should act—and he isn't much of a thinker—and when he finally reverts to the uncivilized self that served him so well, he discovers that his brief sojourn into civilization has blunted his edge. Mrs. Miller is better suited for the fray than any man—McCabe included. But she, bitterly frustrated by a life of being more clever than those who have power over her, chooses escape via opium as her response to any crisis.

Altman's images may seem offhand, as conversational as his dialogue, but they're chosen with care. He and longtime collaborator, cinematographer Vilmos Zsigmund, use a lovely naturalist framing to support an emotionally subjective camera. The constantly moving lens seeks the emotional core of the scene, even if that core is tucked off to the side of what appears to be the main action. The lighting is complicated and, like Altman's dialogue, naturalist; light seems to come only from existing sources: a lantern, a dirty window, a fireplace.

Poetic, visually dazzling, rich in character, philosophical, violent, reverent, and sad; the most European of all westerns.

Other recommended rentals directed by Robert Altman:
Brewster McCloud
Buffalo Bill & the Indians
The Long Goodbye (see page 93)
The Player

The Miracle of Morgan's Creek

Madcap classic **:ATTITUDE**

Relentless screwball comedy **:MOOD**

DIRECTOR: Preston Sturges (1944—U.S.A.)
CAST: Betty Hutton, William Demarest, Eddie Bracken
IN ENGLISH; B/W

William Demarest and Betty Hutton in *The Miracle of Morgan's Creek*

Debunking the sanctity of motherhood, fatherhood, the armed forces, true love, marriage, and the (John Fordian) will of the community, Sturges creates a nonstop anarchy of wit, pace, and style that has lost none of its punch since 1944. The wit is eloquent, the pace is break-neck, and the style is pure Preston Sturges.

Physical comedienne extraordinaire Betty Hutton plays a small-town girl who goes to a farewell dance for hundreds of servicemen leaving for the war. In the course of a wild evening she hits her head, drinks too much, marries a soldier, conceives a baby by him, and wakes up with not a clue as to what happened or, more importantly, to the identity of the soldier-father. Enter Eddie Bracken, Betty's sad-sack pal who's been romancing her in vain for years. He agrees to a fake marriage so she can get the first one annulled, so they can then marry one another for real. As loony as that sounds, things get even loonier.

At the center of this chaos is William Demarest as Betty's father, the local constable and a rock of intransigent courage. He performs physical slapstick with psychotic commitment and complete disregard for orthopedic consequences; he hurls himself into back flips with such ferocity you fear he might break his neck.

Sturges skates across this impossible plot, maintaining his charming, light touch no matter how insane events become. Bracken and Hutton share numerous scenes, their dialogue flying back and forth as fast as possible. Other sequences feature several players talking *over* one another just as quickly. Sturges's usual crew of actors are vocal magicians, and deliver the nonstop verbiage with speed-freak dexterity. The dialogue crackles as the gags range from subtle puns to the most preposterous vaudeville. Some of the gags seem dated, some are side-splitting, and some breathtaking in their audacity.

Racing from joke to joke like a man with his pants on fire, Sturges's exuberance never flags. When the plot turns nonsensical, Sturges ignores it. When events threaten belief, he amps up the slapstick, increases the already frenetic pace, and throws in more jokes. The manic energy keeps you breathlessly awaiting the next plot turn or gag. Sturges digs himself into impossible plot-holes, and the thrill lies in watching him pull himself out.

Sturges's machine-gun repartee may distract you from the genius of his moviemaking. He likes five-minute unbroken tracking shots of Bracken and Hutton yakking back and forth. These shots go on and on, stacking gag on top of gag. It's a high-wire act: an impossible balancing of the actors, the jokes, and the shot itself. Every time it seems he cannot possibly find a new payoff to close a scene, he does. It's spectacular.

Sturges's outlook is both sentimental and deeply cynical. Underlying the relentless absurdities and (almost) happy ending, are his trenchant insights into the repressive morality of a small town, the desperation to conform and to find love, the burdens of heroism, and the short attention span of the condemning or approving public. Among the dizzying aspects is Sturges's own rapidly revolving and contradictory views about everything he presents. You may try to interpret as it all whizzes by, or you may just hold on for the ride, laughing all the way.

Other recommended rentals directed by Preston Sturges:

The Great McGinty

The Lady Eve (see page 84)

Sullivan's Travels

The Missouri Breaks

Modernist western **:ATTITUDE**
Literate, ironic, revisionist revenge-opera **:MOOD**

DIRECTOR: Arthur Penn (1976—U.S.A.)
CAST: Jack Nicholson, Marlon Brando, Harry Dean Stanton, Kathleen
   Lloyd
IN ENGLISH; COLOR

Marlon Brando and Jack Nicholson in *The Missouri Breaks*

Even when indulging his trademark excess of irony, there's no more
subtle nor historically accurate screenwriter of westerns than Thomas
McGuane. With his devout love of self-invented American slang,
McGuane can create a full-blooded character with a single sentence,
and his characters speak like no others in film; they speak like normal
folks. This contributes to McGuane's air of authority and an air of
historically—though never politically—correct style in dress, speech,
and attitude.

   The story showcases a battle between a dwindling outlaw culture
(free enterprise) and the entrenched entrepreneurs (big business) of
the dreaded New West. Jack Nicholson, no slouch at irony himself,
leads a motley cast of horse thieves—seconded by the incomparable

Harry Dean Stanton—locked in mortal combat with a poetry-spouting megarancher. The horse thieves are exceptionally well cast, and feature Frederic Forrest and Randy Quaid.

Marlon Brando appears like an apparition, playing a "regulator": a legalized murderer of rustlers. Marlon keeps things *real* interesting; he is either completely out of his mind or portraying with unholy conviction a man who might be. Jack falls for the rancher's daughter and learns the hard way that if he weren't born with murderous instincts, he'd better grow some. Jack finds himself inadequate to the task, and in his conflicted heart rages the struggle that McGuane sees at the heart of the development of the West: the struggle between violence as an all-purpose problem-solver, and a more sentimental view, one in which hardscrabble homesteads evolve naturally into large-scale land development.

The film, for all its remarkable shoot-outs, action sequences, and one-liners (Randy Quaid: "The closer you get to Canada, the more things there are that eat your horse."), has a delightful, schizophrenic quality. This owes in large part to Brando, who was apparently a nightmare on the set. (He reportedly blackmailed the producer into giving him a mobile home by refusing to learn his lines.) Brando's performance of a wacky manhunter is so relentlessly wacky that he shatters the illusion of watching a movie. When he's on-screen you watch him and everyone else fades away . . . everyone, that is, except Nicholson. In their shared scenes, Brando gets even wackier, but Nicholson holds his ground.

As is usually the case for McGuane heroes, as soon as Nicholson does what's necessary to stay alive, he loses every single thing that makes staying alive worthwhile: home, friends, family, and freedom. The conflict in Nicholson's heart is resolved, and like every other western hero before him, he turns to violence, for which McGuane's characters show sadistic flair. Director Arthur Penn (*Bonnie and Clyde, Little Big Man*) may be unable to control Brando or the plot, but he does understand shoot-outs. The resulting gunfights aren't exactly traditional, but they're fun—and extremely violent.

Lovely scenery, a touching love story, superb acting (especially from Harry Dean Stanton), and the not-uninteresting spectacle of Marlon Brando deliberately destroying himself.

Other recommended rentals directed by Arthur Penn:
Bonnie and Clyde
The Chase (see page 28)
Night Moves

My Darling Clementine

Classic western **:ATTITUDE**
Magnificent character study with gunplay **:MOOD**

DIRECTOR: John Ford (1946—U.S.A.)
CAST: Henry Fonda, Walter Brennan, Victor Mature, Linda Darnell
IN ENGLISH; B/W

Fred Libby, John Ireland, Walter Brennan, Mickey Simpson, Francis Ford, and Grant Withers in *My Darling Clementine*

A John Ford western of mood, character, and cinematography. Compared to the bombastic cartooning of *Fort Apache* or (heresy to some, I know) *The Searchers*, *Clementine* is startlingly modern in its quiet contemplation, dark undercurrents, and unequivocal thematic material. This is Ford's most intelligent, restrained, and purposefully beautiful western. For once, Ford presents violence and romance as a grown-up might perceive them, rather than as backdrops to John Wayne.

The Earp brothers drive their cattle near Tombstone, Arizona. While the elder Earps visit the town, their herd is rustled and their youngest brother killed. Wyatt (Henry Fonda) and his brothers (including Ward Bond in a noble and commanding performance) become town marshals. They discover their nemeses, the Clanton family, led by Walter Brennan as a brooding paternal monarch. Fonda cleans up the town, meets a pretty schoolmarm, and befriends the tubercular Doc Holiday, played in a jarring piece of casting-against-type by Victor Mature. The Earps team up with Doc Holiday and together fight the Clantons at the O.K. Corral.

Shooting in magnificent black-and-white, Ford opens up his frame as never before or since. Almost every exterior shot offers vistas of sky and clouds. Ford uses light and dark with great force and storytelling precision. When Walter Brennan—a study in pure evil—appears, the world becomes all shadows, suggesting the tortured dark canyons of old man Clanton's soul. When Fonda steps onto the floor of a half-built church, tosses off his hat, and dances with the schoolmarm, blinding sunlight shines down on the whole community.

At that moment, Fonda aligns himself with the town (by taking off his hat, symbolic of life on the open range), accepts the continuity of civilizing traditions (by climbing up to the church and acknowledging its power), and commits to living a circumscribed and productive life (by symbolically marrying the schoolmarm in his joyous dance). The moment encapsulates all of Ford's notions of the taming of the West.

With this performance, Henry Fonda defines Wyatt Earp and creates an enduring western heroic archetype: a man of few words but deep integrity, whose superior moral strength is required to civilize the town, just as the town's comforting community is necessary to civilize him.

Brennan, as the vicious head of the Clantons, shows a dark side you may not think he possessed. He plays Clanton as ruthless assassin and pathetic old man. Victor Mature's Doc Holiday is simply strange; his romance with the hellcat Chiquita is a bit embarrassing compared to Earp's stately courting of the ephemeral Clementine. Mature wears one of the least appropriate hats in western history; if you can overlook that, his Doc Holiday almost works.

Compared to Ford's usual gun battles, with their blaring music, whooping Indians, and bugling cavalrymen, the gunfight at the O.K. Corral is hauntingly silent. No music accompanies the violence, which plays to the sound of the desert wind and to boots scuffling in the sand. This sequence shows the master at the top of his form: no sentimentality, no John Wayne, no simple lessons, no life lost—however degraded—without mourning.

A textbook of western values, issues, heroes, and villains. Fifty years later it's still mesmerizing, amusing, and a classic of the form.

Other recommended rentals directed by John Ford:
Fort Apache
The Grapes of Wrath
The Searchers

Near Dark

Vampire biker love :**ATTITUDE**
Gory, funny horror :**MOOD**

DIRECTOR: Kathryn Bigelow (1987—U.S.A.)
CAST: Jenette Goldstein, Lance Henriksen, William Paxton, Adrian Pasdar, Jenny Wright
IN ENGLISH; COLOR

This is an astounding, subversive treatment of a classic theme: love between a vampire and a mortal, set for maximum weirdness in the modern, rural wasteland of Western suburbia. This time the vampire's a girl and the doomed mortal is the boy she loves. Her "daddy," the big-time, bad-ass, biker vampire—god of all character actors Lance Henriksen in full leather—opposes their love match unless certain changes are made regarding the boy's status as a mortal. The girl finds herself torn between mortal love and vampire loyalty, while the boy tries to avoid finding himself torn, period. His adopted family of the undead discovers numerous, sadistic methods of pressuring him into making the final leap from human to bloodsucker. As they work on our hero, his "blood" relatives relentlessly pursue the vampires across a bleak landscape of truck stops and minimalls.

Director Kathryn Bigelow (*Blue Steel, Strange Days*) has since moved on to less interesting, big-studio projects. Back when she was a struggling, low-budget visionary, her obsession with sex and style found voice in this grainy, violent gem. Henriksen plays the hundred-year-old head vampire with a gleam in his eye and pure malice in his heart. It's the first in his ten-year run of stellar villains (culminating in *Hard Target*), and the bloodiest of them all. Bill Paxton plays a dumb-ass hick vampire who is happy to fight for his right to party—and to rape, maim, and suck blood. Bigelow's scenes of the vampires amuck in some poor Southwest township had no equal for barbarous, side-splitting violence until Travolta stuck that syringe into Uma's chest in *Pulp Fiction*. And, like Tarantino, Bigelow does not lack commitment when it's time to spill blood. The gallons that pour make the humor more earned, less exploitative, but don't ask me how.

Bigelow's approach is Tarantinoish in more ways than blood-drenched humor. Like Tarantino, she understands that ironic action-fests live or die by their pacing: lulls are fatal. So, there are none.

The story races like an ostrich on speed, and if vampires aren't tearing a town apart or tormenting our hero, then the hero and his undead sweetie are making love. Adrian Pasdar and Jenny Wright play the star-crossed lovers. Both are easy on the eyes—if not the most gifted actors—so the less they wear and the less they say, the better.

You might be able to predict the story, but you'll still be amazed at the bloody élan, sex appeal, swell motorcycles, ripping car chases, imaginative gunplay, ardent teenage love, and overall gripping atmosphere that emerges from what should have been low-budget trash, but is redeemed by wit and imagination.

Perfect casting, perfect over-the-top acting, and more blood than three slaughterhouses. But that's no surprise, right? What's a vampire picture, ironic or not, without buckets of blood?

92 in the Shade

Irony-fest in Key West :**ATTITUDE**
Wacky, talky, absurdist comedy :**MOOD**

DIRECTOR: Thomas McGuane (1975—U.S.A.)
CAST: Peter Fonda, Warren Oates, Margot Kidder, Burgess Meredith
IN ENGLISH; COLOR

Peter Fonda and Warren Oates in *92 in the Shade*

Thomas McGuane, screenwriter of *Tom Horn* (see page 173), *Rancho Deluxe* (page 139) and *The Missouri Breaks* (page 107), directed only one film, but he made the most of his opportunity. Adapting his own offbeat novel, shooting in his adopted home of Key West, McGuane creates a nutcase little universe with a cast to kill for: Peter Fonda, Warren Oates, Margot Kidder, Burgess Meredith, Harry Dean Stanton, Elizabeth Ashley, Sylvia Miles, and Joe Spinell. Yes, the set was a hipster's paradise, a bunch of crazy pals making a crazy movie while going crazy. Several marriages supposedly foundered on the rocks of this production, McGuane's and Fonda's among them.

McGuane is a writer, not a filmmaker. He has no evident moviemaking skills except the ability to befriend the best character actors on the planet. The visuals are offhand, the colors are rich and tropical, the pace languid, the cinema nonexistent, but the language, sublime.

"He had a hoochie-coochie from Opa Locka and *she* thought *he* was dumb!" Burgess Meredith tells Peter Fonda, who appears appropriately baffled. Fonda's special brand of nonacting has seldom been so well employed.

Fonda, playing a benign if aimless young adult (Existential Malaise alert!), decides, for lack of a better purpose, to become a fishing guide in Key West. The immortal Warren Oates, already established as a guide, doesn't want the competition; if Fonda goes through with his plan Oates promises to kills him.

Peter's crazy father (acting coach William Hickey) tries to discourage him. His overbearing grandpa (Burgess Meredith) wants to help. Wills clash. Tempers rise. Trailer-Park America—in the form of Elizabeth Ashley as an aging baton twirler and Harry Dean Stanton as her put-upon husband—pitches a fit. Peter and Warren become buddies, though neither will back down. The climax of their struggle depends on whether you rent the director's cut, which the studio did not release, or the studio version, which the director despises. The two differ only in the final sixty seconds.

That the studio went to war over the ending is absurd. Any film this eccentric, literate, and formless hadn't a prayer of mainstream success anyway. Happily, every quality that guaranteed box-office doom twenty years ago makes this shambling fable a treasure today: dark, daring wit (a McGuane specialty), stellar understated performances, and the director's gift for capturing American rhythms of speech.

Among McGuane's fascinations is the minute aesthetics that develop around manly, skill-based recreation, particularly fishing and hunting. Nobody captures so insightfully the tiny heartfelt snobberies that mark the world of such endeavors. Treating these snobberies as the entirely male psychoses that they are, McGuane incorporates into his screenplay lessons in the proper manly attitudes and behavior, and how men might die for violating either. McGuane mocks, but he's as serious about his fishing as Hemingway. His seriousness grants the farcical competition between Fonda and Oates its believable and essential homicidal edge.

Is it a deadpan comedy, a meditation on fate, or a low-key work of art? More likely it's a cult film for adults: smart, loose, funny, and too ironic for its own good.

Out of the Blue

. . . And into the black :**ATTITUDE**
Dark, brutal drama :**MOOD**

DIRECTOR: Dennis Hopper (1980—Canada)
CAST: Dennis Hopper, Linda Manz, Don Gordon, Sharon Farrell
IN ENGLISH; COLOR

Only Dennis Hopper would kill a whole schoolbus full of children just to make his character sympathetic—and that prior to the opening credits! Hopper had been neither rehabilitated in the eyes of Hollywood nor turned into self-parody when he directed this bleak neorealist ode to sheer hopelessness.

However deeply Hopper was into madness or drugs or what*ever*, he knew how to return from the depths of hell and report what he had seen. Hopper managed the difficult task of maintaining narrative drive while connecting to, and accurately depicting, crippling emotional torment. If that sounds like a European art film, it shouldn't. Hopper is working in very American territory: the tortures of the working class. And, however harrowing this journey, it's worth every step.

Told through the eyes of the lovely, blank-faced, New York–accented Linda Manz (*Days of Heaven*), the tale follows Hopper's character as he emerges from prison, reunites with his wife and teenage daughter (Manz), and attempts to remake a life in the small town he denuded of children so long ago. Hopper plays a man who cannot get out of his own way and everyone around him looks to self-immolate with a desperation equal to his own. Manz reacts by withdrawing into a shell of punk rebellion: doing dope, pounding on drums, and hating her parents, who are, admittedly, hateful.

It's a scorching portrait of dysfunctional family life, love, and infidelity (and the infidelity is *red hot*), the terrors of not having enough money, and the horror of having no escape from anything, your own demons included. Hopper lacked the budget for fancy camera work, so there isn't any. The look of the film is clean and simple, and dominated by deep, deep blues. Often the camera sits still for minutes at a time, the better to showcase the emotional carnage. Hopper focused on the acting, which is phenomenal. He chose a realistic, improvisational style, so his actors' dialogue and cadences have a true-to-life, stuttering quality. There are few films with acting so superb, yet so raw. Hopper's own scenes might ramble occasionally, and the pacing is not slick, but the force of the story never lags even when the storytelling might.

Few directors can take on this kind of emotional wreckage without succumbing to melodrama. Bergman's *Scenes from a Marriage* comes to mind, but even that depicted the materially rosy circumstances of a protected, professional couple. Hopper's film begins with economic and emotional calamity and things only get worse. The clarity of Hopper's vision, his belief in the certainty of doom, and the subtlety of the performances makes this an illuminating, down-and-out masterpiece.

Extremely smart, instinctive, and visceral filmmaking, one of the fine and enduring little-known pictures of the last fifteen years. Rent it when you are feeling particularly strong or particularly down. Either way, it will only give you strength.

Other recommended rentals directed by Dennis Hopper:
Colors
Easy Rider
The Last Movie (see page 86)

Out of the Past

Noir apotheosis **:ATTITUDE**
Gripping, profound, suspense-thriller **:MOOD**

DIRECTOR: Jacques Tourneur (1947—U.S.A.)
CAST: Robert Mitchum, Kirk Douglas, Jane Greer, Jack Elam
IN ENGLISH; B/W

Virginia Huston and Robert Mitchum in *Out of the Past*

Screenwriter Daniel Mainwaring wrote *Invasion of the Body Snatchers*. Cinematographer Nick Musuraca shot the surreal *Cat People*. Director Jacques Tourneur's approach—in fact his life—was noir incarnate. These B-movie all-stars combine to create a classic: a bleak, enthralling tale of a man struggling to escape his fate even as he knows he is utterly and deservedly doomed.

Robert Mitchum plays a hoodlum dragged out of self-imposed exile by mobster Kirk Douglas to track down Douglas's runaway girlfriend, the fatally seductive Jane Greer. Even as Mitchum recognizes the mortal danger of falling for her, he does. Even as Mitchum knows he's being played for a chump, he rushes into the flames. Does he condemn himself out of profane love, a yearning for redemption, weariness of life, or sheer perversity? As you might have guessed, all of the above. Douglas has never seemed so evil, nor has he so reveled in his own physique. He swells with menace when confronting Mitchum, and his final threats to Jane Greer are downright terrifying.

Director Tourneur's sense of hopelessness and existential dread—hard-earned during a hardly lucrative career that featured seminal but underappreciated work like *I Walked with a Zombie*—find expression in a desolate compendium of noir characteristics: violence, sexual obsession, alienation, betrayal, and (justified) paranoia, all presented in eerie, shadow-laden lighting, and dreamlike camera work. Everyone betrays; some for love, some for money, some out of boredom. For spooky directorial flourishes amid a hopelessly confusing (and ultimately unimportant) plot, this film has no equal. Nor for black-and-white cinematography, acting, or soul.

Mitchum's alienation is key; he's alienated from himself, from sacred love, and, by his betrayals, even from his own kind: gangsters. In typical noir fashion, Mitchum never "blames" Kirk Douglas for his troubles. He recognizes the villain as nothing more than an actualizer of evil forces long extant in the world of men, and in his own psyche. Mitchum's only faith is his absolute lack of faith, his conviction that things will worsen no matter what course he follows. No other actor could present such knowing resignation when confronted with the absurd universe of his own folly. Mitchum shines, sappy as a schoolboy in love one moment, psychotically violent the next, with never a contradiction apparent.

Jane Greer, likewise, is the classic noir femme fatale: the embodiment of sexual terror, a seducer-destroyer, smarter than any man but needy, too—she not only outwits you, she steals your heart as well. No woman in noir is sexually active without being destructive, and Greer's character is no exception. She's both—and damn compelling either way.

One of the all-timers: fierce, poetic, suspenseful, complex, intelligent, heartbreaking, and lovely to gaze upon. A happy ending? I don't think so. . . .

Other recommended rentals directed by Jacques Tourneur:
Cat People (1942)
I Walked with a Zombie
Night of the Demon

The Outsiders

Melodramatic teendom :**ATTITUDE**
Star-powered arty drama, with fistfights :**MOOD**

DIRECTOR: Francis Ford Coppola (1983—U.S.A.)
CAST: Matt Dillon, Rob Lowe, Patrick Swayze, C. Thomas Howell,
    Ralph Macchio
IN ENGLISH; COLOR

The cast includes Matt Dillon, C. Thomas Howell, Tom Cruise, Rob Lowe, Patrick Swayze, Ralph Macchio, Emilio Estevez, and former teen idol Leif Garrett as well as Coppola regulars Diane Lane and Tom Waits. Coppola shot *Rumble Fish* (see page 149) in sequence with *The Outsiders,* one after the other, on location in Tulsa, Oklahoma. Both are his collaborative adaptions of S. E. Hinton's best-selling young-adult novels.

Coppola said he wanted to make *"Gone with the Wind* for teenagers," and he succeeded wildly. This deliberately overwrought saga of the eternal teen search for identity plays out against a background of small-town class war in the early 1960s. Coppola exaggerates colors—which he alters to underline the emotional valence of every moment—to the point of hallucination. He also references every teen movie ever made, with a particular nod to *Rebel Without a Cause,* another film that used color to indicate the tortured emotional swings of adolescence.

Dillon, Macchio, and Howell are best buddies and "greasers"—lower-class kids who wear jeans and T-shirts and who put Elvis-style grease in their hair. Their sworn enemies are the "socs"—rich kids who wear khakis and drive Mustangs. A soc dies in a knife fight and our trio runs away. While on the lam, one of them becomes a hero, thus enabling the others to return. But Dillon's love for Diane Lane, a soc to the nth degree, causes trouble. A huge rumble results, after which Dillon is pursued by the cops. In reaching the tragic finale, both greasers and socs openly acknowledge what they always pretended to ignore: that their economic status points them to very different kinds of lives. Their rumbles are the only time they can meet as equals.

Where *Rumble Fish* concerns a search for glory, here Coppola presents something much more basic: the nature of teenage love—the stumbling love between boys and girls, the intense, reflexive, never-mentioned love between boys and boys. Coppola also delivers a world without adults, where the only concerns are teen concerns: urgency, loyalty, a glandular need for violence, and the implicit power to star in one's own mythology. While celebrating their world, Coppola evinces a powerful nostalgia for the days of such simple problems.

Whether teenagers will actually enjoy this movie is another question. The shifts in color, or to dramatic close-up, are only part of Coppola's subjective cinema. Representing the agitated nature of adolescence, he brings an embarrassing level of emotion to every little moment. His camera also gazes with frank adoration at the handsome young faces of his stars. This approach is jarring, until you recognize Coppola's intention: He's showing the world not as these kids see it, but as they feel it.

In his naked connection to those feelings, this is Coppola's most courageous work. Though ridiculed upon release, *The Outsiders* stands as a deeply emotional, personal piece of filmmaking. There's an inescapable sense of tragedy throughout. The climactic rumble—fought in a rainstorm under such blue light that the picture turns almost black-and-white—demonstrates Coppola's abilities as a director of both action and emotion.

Somehow connecting to an American naiveté he has long since outgrown, Coppola brings a European-art-film sensibility to a subject only an American could ever understand.

Other recommended rentals directed by Francis Ford Coppola:

Apocalypse Now
The Conversation
The Godfather Parts I and II
Rumble Fish (see page 149)

The Passenger

Existential travelogue avec suspense **:ATTITUDE**
Arty, profound, compelling riddle **:MOOD**

DIRECTOR: Michelangelo Antonioni (1975—Italy/France/Spain)
CAST: Jack Nicholson, Maria Schneider, Jenny Runacre
IN ENGLISH; COLOR

Jack Nicholson in *The Passenger*

Tired of his own habits, bored out of his mind, alone in the wilderness, Jack Nicholson commits a desperate act and lives life on the run. Just *whose* life he's living is not exactly clear, but the point is the living itself.

Nicholson plays a journalist who can no longer stand the sound of his own voice or the consequences of his actions. A quirk of fate enables him to swap identities with a dead man. Despite the drastic changes this move creates, in the end Jack's problem turns out to be that no matter where you go, there you are.

While the burdens of Nicholson's misspent life are purely existential—self-loathing, inertia, the end of enthusiasm—those of his doppelgänger are life-threatening. The threads of Jack's old life and of his new intertwine, and he finds no escape from either world. Antonioni shows his hero no more pity than he shows the rest of the cast—that is, none—and yet the result remains uplifting, almost religious, and unforgettable. Antonioni has no faith in the fairness of life, but he shows a connoisseur's interest in its process.

Maria Schneider (*Last Tango in Paris*) joins Nicholson via coincidence—everything happens via coincidence—and together they flee across Europe, moving through the lyrical wide-screen landscape as only Antonioni could perceive it—as poetic, nourishing, and not at all interested in the problems of living souls.

While this is Antonioni's most accessible film, it moves with the director's typically graceful torpor, and patience is required. The plot, for an Antonioni film, is unusually straightforward. In *Blow-Up*, the story served as a vehicle for a study of character and culture. Here the plot (the screenplay was cowritten by Mark Peploe, who cowrote *The Last Emperor* with Bernardo Bertolucci) resembles a traditional story, with suspense, love scenes, and even a chase sequence of sorts.

The final seven minutes of the film comprise one famous unbroken take, a single shot of breathtaking complexity and narrative drive, even though the slowest of snails could outrun the camera as it moves. And if you can't—or choose not to—follow the story, the film is so beautiful . . .

Suspenseful, magnificent, aware of itself as cinema every second, and yet not pretentious. Okay, not all *that* pretentious.

Other recommended rentals directed by Michelangelo Antonioni:
L'Avventura
Blow-Up
Red Desert
Zabriskie Point

Pat Garrett & Billy the Kid

Peckinpah's farewell western **:ATTITUDE**
Lovely, tragic, violent western **:MOOD**

DIRECTOR: Sam Peckinpah (1973—U.S.A.)
CAST: Kris Kristofferson, James Coburn, Bob Dylan, Slim Pickens
IN ENGLISH; COLOR

L.Q. Jones and James Coburn in *Pat Garrett & Billy the Kid*

Sam Peckinpah made the greatest western of all time, *The Wild Bunch;* maybe the finest American film ever. While this is not Peckinpah's final picture, it feels like a farewell, and to the western, it is. After re-defining the genre with *Ride the High Country,* he purposely wrecked forever the credibility of the traditional western with *The Wild Bunch.* In *Pat Garrett,* Peckinpah returns to the turf he knows best to pro-duce a moving, poetic, and tragic summing-up of both the Old West and his own career.

Kris Kristofferson is Billy the Kid, doomed to be betrayed by his former best friend, Marshall Pat Garrett, played by James Coburn. Bob Dylan, in his feature debut, plays the enigmatic Alias. His mock-profound role should be irritating, but Bob's willingness to take a back-seat is positively endearing. The supporting cast comprises an American Who's Who of western character actors—Harry Dean Stanton, L.Q. Jones, Luke Askew, Slim Pickens, Chill Wills, Richard Jaeckel, Jason Robards, Jack Elam, R.G. Armstrong, and even Katy Jurado, who costarred in *High Noon*—all assembled for their inherently mythic as well as dramatic qualities. (The only ones missing are Ben Johnson, Warren Oates, Charles Bronson, Dub Taylor, and Strother Martin.)

Everyone is appropriately scraggly; the hippie aesthetic had invaded Hollywood to the point that *Pat Garrett* features a cast with the most historically accurate range of hair lengths of any western. Taking advantage of all that hair, Peckinpah turns the struggle between Billy and Pat into a war between the free-spirited long-hairs and the repressive, daddylike straights. As a device, it's intermittently successful.

Peckinpah self-consciously raises themes that remain metaphorical in his earlier pictures: themes of the pointlessness of honor in the modern world, the closing of the West at the hands of corrupt bureaucrats, and—Peckinpah's favorite—that every man must destroy the aspect of himself he most loves in order to survive in the adult world. At times the presentation of these themes seems heavy-handed, at other times sublime in its subtlety. As in every Peckinpah film, the action sequences—with their transcendent violence, mixture of motion speeds, multiple camera positions, and complex editing—are a revelation.

Peckinpah chooses a sentimental, blue-laden light to suggest the end of a way of life. Each violent sequence kills off another archetype of the old ways: the crusty sheriff, the independent rustlers, or the free-agent bounty hunter. While the first three-quarters of the film features Peckinpah's self-indulgent cornball, his inexcusable misogyny, and some rather obvious mythmaking, the last half hour is the finest western—in pacing, acting, camera work, dialogue, editing, music, gunfights, mood, atmosphere, historical accuracy, and meaningful legend-mongering—ever made.

The sound track, written and performed by Dylan, greatly enhances the fin de siècle air of tragedy, of a glory lost never to be regained. The album of this sound track, *Pat Garrett & Billy the Kid*, remains Dylan's forgotten masterwork. In its heartfelt air of romantic melancholy, it's the perfect companion to the film.

Other recommended rentals directed by Sam Peckinpah:
Cross of Iron
Major Dundee
Straw Dogs
The Wild Bunch

Paths of Glory

Antiwar war movie **:ATTITUDE**
Cinematic courtroom/war drama **:MOOD**

DIRECTOR: Stanley Kubrick (1957—U.S.A.)
CAST: Kirk Douglas, Adolphe Menjou, Timothy Carey, Ralph Meeker
IN ENGLISH; B/W

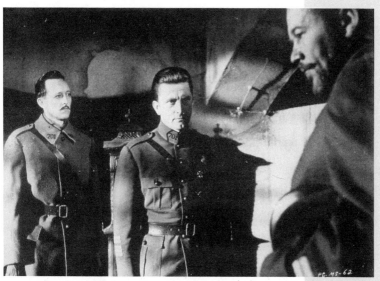

Kirk Douglas and Wayne Morris in *Paths of Glory*

Kubrick finds in war movies a vehicle for his favorite themes: the hopelessness of man's nature, the evils of war, and the murderous, self-serving nature of any entrenched hierarchy. War movies also enable Kubrick to work out his fascination with the sexiness of ritualized/

mechanized death and with the foolish, serpentine rituals that men create.

Kirk Douglas stars as a World War I French infantry commander who leads an ill-considered assault against a German fortress, and later must serve as defense counsel in a vain attempt to keep three of his soldiers from the firing squad. Ralph Meeker gives the performance of his career—the only deeply felt, multileveled character he ever played—as one of the doomed soldiers. Kubrick's regulars play the other condemned men, quirky actors whom other directors seldom employed: Joseph Turkel and Timothy Carey.

Carey, one of the most memorable characters in movies, walks, as always, his own special tightrope between instinctual actor and charismatic sociopath. Naturalist and hyperreal, the essence of Carey's craft is displaying no craft at all. He radiates a complex, idiot-savant combination of naiveté and cunning. His willingness to display craven cowardice is horrible to behold, both for the character and for the courage of an actor who could so connect to his worst aspects within. His performance must be seen to be believed. It's so strange, so moving; Carey justifies the rental price all by himself.

Kubrick shows remarkable maturity—and no small amount of uncharacteristic arty self-consciousness—as a director, moving the camera in constant backward or forward tracking shots. Shooting in wide angle, the knee-level camera—the precursor to Kubrick's groundbreaking Steadicam work in *The Shining*—brings a dramatic sense of inexorable fate. It also makes the war action exciting as hell.

Kubrick reminds us always of the larger narrative setting—be it trenches, elegant ballrooms, or palace gardens rigged for a firing squad—by shooting with a superwide-angle lens. Wisely—and showing a staggering range of technique—Kubrick abandons tracking shots for the courtroom sequence. There he alternates between a superwide master shot and supertight close-ups. His ability to simultaneously underscore both the dramatic and moral dynamics of every scene mark him even this early in his career. This particular gift will reappear in more polished form in *Dr. Strangelove*.

Kubrick's cynicism never found more balanced expression. The finale suggests that Kubrick once believed that man's goopy sentimentality might rescue him from his native barbarism. In his later films, *A Clockwork Orange, Barry Lyndon* (see page 10), and *The Shining,* Kubrick abandoned faith even in that pathetic aspect of the species. Back then, Kubrick was still capable of compassion, and his hero emerges as a moral and worthy figure. Kubrick's pitiless later films feature heroes who deserve every punishment they receive, or no heroes at all.

A moving antiwar statement, exciting war action, a superb star turn from Kirk Douglas, riveting courtroom dynamics, and a stunning visual style from a budding master. Kubrick sought to make a Big Theme picture and he succeeds where so many others have failed.

How? By never swallowing nor concealing a single moral ambiguity and by following the dictum of Howard Hawks: "Big ideas are hogwash. Just tell the story."

Other recommended rentals directed by Stanley Kubrick:
2001: A Space Odyssey
Barry Lyndon (see page 10)
A Clockwork Orange
Dr. Strangelove or: How I Learned to Stop Worrying and Love the Bomb
Full Metal Jacket
The Killing
Lolita (see page 91)

Peeping Tom

Voyeuristic weirdness **:ATTITUDE**
1950s-style psychosexual thriller **:MOOD**

DIRECTOR: Michael Powell (1960—U.K.)
CAST: Moira Shearer, Karl Böhm, Anna Massey
IN ENGLISH; COLOR

Michael Powell's *Peeping Tom*

Michael Powell, apparently tired of being oblique, wrote and directed this exercise in sadism and irresistible compulsion. Upon release, the film seemed a willful act of subversion designed to undo all of Powell's credibility, and it damn near succeeded. Once a banned scandal, it's now rightly regarded as a classic: a film with the guts to name the unnamable, an obsessive portrait of obsession. It is filmed without mercy for the hero, the director, or the audience. And written with a cold, misanthropic wit to rival Mark Twain's.

What many mistook as a straightforward paean to the worst urges of man is actually a rather heartbreaking tale of an innocent gone awry, a gentle soul turned horrible by vicious paternal attentions—attentions detailed in nightmarish flashbacks. Those familiar with Powell's sense of humor will not be surprised that Powell himself plays the terrible daddy.

The protagonist is a murderer of women, who kills with a movie camera to which he has attached a long knife and a big mirror—representing Sex and Self-consciousness, respectively. He stabs his victims and films them as they watch themselves die in the mirror. Naturally, being a filmmaker, our murderer's true pleasure lies not in murder nor even in filming, but in watching the film later. It's a commentary on the voyeurism and the power of cinema, a telling parable about the relationship between filmer and filmed, and it's packed with more kooky strangeness than three Coen Brothers pictures combined.

It is told in the bright, clear hues of Technicolor—not a single shadow in this whole shadowy tale—at a pace suitable for a cough-syrup addict. It's not for the squeamish, though it is perversely funny, in its own awful way. Also quite prescient in its prediction of a society dominated by the idea that watching something equals controlling it.

The scenes of the killer running the footage of his murders launched a thousand dumber horror movies (and three or four dazzling ones, like *Manhunter*) but Powell cared not about similarities between his and lesser works. He had a message regarding compulsion to deliver, and deliver it he did, without compromise. Underlying the carnage is quite a moral lesson in the responsibilities of pointing a camera. And, as in all of Powell's films, every technical aspect is simply perfect.

Varied and amusing subtexts for the film sophisticate and, it must be said, plenty of cheap thrills for the horror junkie.

Other recommended rentals directed by Michael Powell and/or Emeric Pressburger :

49th Parallel (see page 51)
Black Narcissus (see page 19)
I Know Where I'm Going (see page 68)
The Life and Times of Colonel Blimp
The Red Shoes
The Small Back Room
Theif of Bagdad (1940; see page 172)

Performance

1970s bong-think mysticism :**ATTITUDE**
Strange, circular, psychedelic thriller :**MOOD**

DIRECTOR: Nicolas Roeg (1970—U.K.)
CAST: Mick Jagger, James Fox, Anita Pallenberg
IN ENGLISH; COLOR

Mick Jagger and Anita Pallenberg in *Performance*

Nicolas Roeg's (*Don't Look Now*) directorial debut is a rock 'n' roll fable on the uncertainty of self and the uneasy friendship between madness and art.

A murderous, uptight English mafia enforcer (James Fox)—he's all action, no soul—needs a hideout. He stumbles upon Mick Jagger's wiggy, Moroccan-tapestried, rich-hippie mansion. Jagger plays a faded rock recluse rendered a hermit by the loss of the inner fire that made him a star: He's all soul, no will. Mick Jagger described this role as "a projection of the producer's fantasy of who he thinks I think I really am."

Jagger sees in James Fox's vicious gangster the demon(s) he's lost. James—experiencing overpowering attraction/revulsion to the sinister free-love capering that includes Anita Pallenberg as the most beautiful woman in the world—sees in Jagger the freedom of expression he craves. Gradually, through inspired crosscutting and knife-edged dialogue, Jagger and Fox recognize their common ground and merge identities altogether. Or do they?

Jagger stars for the one director who knew how to use him. His performance is mesmerizing. Roeg shoots in oversaturated colors and edits as if in a dream. Shifting time and space to emphasize a momentary emotion, a fly on the wall, or a barely overheard conversation, Roeg makes no particular effort to be understood. The plot unravels one clue at a time, as all good mysteries should, and if you miss a clue, you can always revel in the freaky London atmosphere, circa 1969. It's a trippy film, and shocking in its day: Jagger nude, Jagger and Pallenberg romping with an androgynous playmate, free and easy consumption of psychedelics . . . and the kaleidoscopic editing that only makes the experience more, well, trippy.

But for all the film's long-haired trappings, Roeg hardly endorses the hippie ethos. Pallenberg's character believes that as James Fox loosens up (he takes drugs, engages in free love, and learns to dress freaky) his tender virtues will emerge triumphant—the basic hippie credo. Jagger, more cunning and attuned to the dark side, understands that the countercultural trappings are only that. Underneath the long hair, Fox remains unchanged: He's a nasty piece of work. Intrigued by Fox's readiness to violence, Jagger respects him for his commitment to "performance," for his willingness to go all the way in the service of his demons. Jagger evokes those demons, and therein lies the tale.

Roeg allows Jagger to perform only a couple of songs, and neither are simple musical interludes. Just as everything in this 3-D puzzle interconnects on several different levels, so do the songs tell us about Jagger, his relationship with Fox, and how all three are constantly changing. The songs function as an apt, enigmatic Greek chorus, and how much they reveal becomes clearer on a second viewing.

In what may be the first-ever rock video, Mick sings the Stones classic "Memo from Turner," all dolled up as James Fox's worst nightmare: a Teddy Boy gangster of uncertain sexual orientation. The sequence is unforgettable—Jagger's command of himself, his ability to alter his image, to lose himself in "performance" is frightening. Earlier, Jagger plucks a funereal boogie on an acoustic guitar and howls out John Lee Hooker's "Jesse James Blues." It's eerie, sexy, and cool, just like the film.

Mind-blowing in more ways than one.

Other recommended rentals directed by Nicholas Roeg:
Bad Timing
Don't Look Now (see page 43)
The Man Who Fell to Earth

Poto & Cabengo

Absurdity in the heartland :**ATTITUDE**
Quirky, deadpan documentary :**MOOD**

DIRECTOR: Jean-Pierre Gorin (1979—West Germany/France)
IN ENGLISH; COLOR

Like Errol Morris when he made *Gates of Heaven* (see page 53), Director Jean-Pierre Gorin was pursuing one subject for his documentary when, to his surprise, he discovered another. The former: twin sisters who seem to have invented their own language. The latter: the life and delusions of the downward-spiraling American working-class family.

The title derives from the pet names the girls invent for one another. The girls are cute as buttons as they babble in their incomprehensible tongue and try to please their loving but hapless parents. Gorin brings in language scholars, newspaper clippings, and psychologists, all to demonstrate how rare it would be, how unprecedented in language research and history, if these girls indeed had created an unknown speech. Gorin also presents a few nutcase Southern Californians who believe the girls are aliens, or at least that aliens taught them their language.

Gorin has some nasty fun at the expense of these dreamers, displaying an arrogant amusement at the credulity of certain Americans. This is Gorin's only lapse in compassion. Recovering, he makes his points about class war in America, ruthlessly demonstrating how the working-class parents and their friends are hoping for an exotic explanation: a new language, alien abduction, whatever. If there were such an explanation, Gorin shows that might invest their sad lives with something special.

Turns out, to the chagrin of Gorin and the deep disappointment of the parents, that the girls haven't invented a language after all. As the air runs out of that balloon, and entertainingly so, Gorin shifts his focus. First, he explains to the viewer how frustrating it is for him as a filmmaker to come so far only to find no conclusion for his film; it's a striking and prophetic postmodern moment in documentary history.

Gorin turns his camera to the deepening plight of the parents, who have little money, no prospects, and an apparently bottomless reservoir of joviality, regardless. The father finds the girls' apparent normality devastating; his plans to make a fortune on the talk-show or university-research circuit are smashed. No matter, he's a good-hearted guy, and has a dozen other ridiculous ideas to save his family. Gorin brings genuine sympathy to the dad's plight, but he's also enough of a filmmaker to capture every second of the father's rising and inevitably dashed hopes.

The revealing moment occurs when the father practices his real-estate-salesman pitch on his wife. She takes over the conversation, going on and on about the perfect house, describing with big bright eyes and an optimistic smile the dream home she will never have. It's almost too much to bear.

The camera work is straightforward; Gorin likes long takes and the fractured rhythm of conversation. He never breaks an emotional moment into sound bites. His patience forces us to deal with the same issue of too-great intimacy with his subjects that Gorin faced in the filming. The family is so willing to expose themselves to the camera, and apparently unaware of how much it really sees. . . .

Gorin's years as an assistant to Jean-Luc Godard (*Contempt;* see page 32) prepared him for any conceptual situation; he finds lessons in this strange family. Some lessons are complex and have to do with film itself, some are simple and pertain to the beauty and horror of inextinguishable hope. Combining these lessons in a Moebius strip of horror, compassion, and bemusement, Gorin creates a dialogue between filmmaker and subject, between filmmaker and audience, and between the filmmaker and himself.

Other recommended self-conscious modern documentaries:
Sherman's March (directed by Ross McElwee)

Predator

Superior mindless trash :**ATTITUDE**
Noisy, violent adventure :**MOOD**

DIRECTOR: John McTiernan (1987—U.S.A.)
CAST: Arnold Schwarzenegger, Bill Duke, Carl Weathers, Jesse Ventura, Kevin Peter Hall
IN ENGLISH; COLOR

Great violent trash has a sense of itself as such, with no delusions of grandeur. It pays homage to trash aesthetics—violent interludes appearing with metronomic regularity, reasonable but not overdone gestures toward character development, just enough plot for events to occur in sequence, a hobbyist's delight in armament—but aspires to something more. Great trash wallows in the gutter while gazing at the stars.

And this is stellar trash.

Arnold Schwarzenegger plays the toughest of mercenaries who leads his demographically correct platoon—a big scary white guy, a big scary Native American, two medium-sized sinister white guys, and a really big, really scary black guy—into a Latin American jungle on the flimsiest of plot pretexts. The evil U.S. bureaucrat who authorizes the operation is Stallone's *Rocky* nemesis, Carl Weathers. Weathers, like everyone else in the picture, apparently pumped a lot of iron whilst hanging on the set with Schwarzenegger. He and the rest of the cast are jacked up like action toys on steroids; not an arm or a neck doesn't bulge like a Christmas sausage. Even their ears have muscles.

The camera lingers fetishistically over every veiny bicep, as it lingers over every inch of gleaming, oil-slicked weaponry. All that weight-lifting and all those machine guns do the guys little good in the end: They're tracked by an invisible being who tears them to pieces one by one until it's time for the inevitable showdown with Schwarzenegger.

McTiernan, who went on to direct *Die Hard,* has more than enough wit for the enterprise. He moves his camera with energy, and shows a rare understanding of the visual dynamics of multi-camera, multistunt shoot-outs. There's not a single unimaginative action sequence in a picture comprised of little else. The adolescent male-bonding that dominates the few nonviolent minutes dares a little self-parody, but no dialogue is stupid enough to make you groan.

Actors, director, cinematographer, prop guys, special effects—the quality of the production might be explained by everyone making a final dues-paying effort before moving into the upper echelons of Hollywood. Bill Duke gives a tender performance as a psychotic machine-gunner. His next project would be directing the immortal *Deep Cover* (see page 36). Jesse "The Body" Ventura, a pro wrestler so pumped he seems directly connected to an air compressor, also plays a psychotic machine-gunner. He first denies the evil menace stalking the platoon, then gives over entirely to paranoia. It's fun watching him go nuts.

Schwarzenegger shows a rare light touch, mocking his character while wallowing in the liberating gore and phallic machine-gun fire-fights. He gives his all, while communicating that this sort of role is beneath him. Only it isn't—this role is precisely on his level. It's the sort of movie from which Schwarzenegger never should have strayed. A remorseless, unpretentious action-fest, in which everyone involved cares about the quality of the final product more than about screen-time, close-ups, or even money.

Blood, outer-space stuff, and more blood. Not for girls, not for kids. It's boy-time unchained.

Prince of the City

No good deed goes unpunished **:ATTITUDE**
Gripping, cynical police drama **:MOOD**

DIRECTOR: Sidney Lumet (1981—U.S.A.)
CAST: Treat Williams, Jerry Orbach, Bob Balaban, Lindsay
    Crouse
IN ENGLISH; COLOR

Treat Williams in *Prince of the City*

A dark, dramatic, and at times agonizing study of the corrupt universe of New York City cops, district attorneys, crooks, and mobsters, as seen through the eyes of one tormented soul who decides to confess everything and brings the wrath of the whole interlocking structure down upon his head.

Directed by New York cop–crook movie avatar Sidney Lumet (*Serpico, Dog Day Afternoon*) and based on a true story, *Prince* follows Treat Williams as a cop in an elite squad of crimefighters who make more arrests and secure more convictions than any other squad in the city. They also steal money and drugs from those they bust. Williams—a working-class cop from the outer boroughs—is driven by the potent dualities of giant ego/self-loathing plus a heroic urge/class inferiority, and lets himself be seduced by two white-bread Manhattan D.A.s. They flatter him over his own importance and the importance of their crusade against police corruption; Williams trusts them and informs on his partners.

The response to his supposed heroism is hardly the laurels he anticipates. He is made an outcast, the Mafia tries to kill him, some of his partners go to jail, and others attempt suicide rather than face the shame. Williams watches, appalled, as the corruption cases created by his testimony labor through the bureaucratic swamp; his D.A. protectors get plush new assignments and move up the ladder. New D.A.s break long-standing deals and treat him not as a hero, but as a snitch. The confusion depresses him to the point of suicidal folly.

Lumet explored this territory in *Serpico* and *Q & A*, but in those melodramas he never addressed the pervasive ambiguity of the life of cops. Here contradictions rule the day: Mafiosos offer to save Williams's life and cops try to kill him. The high-minded white upper-class lawyers, D.A.s, and judges lie to Williams as they pursue career advancement. Meanwhile, ethnic working-class cops and crooks offer Williams loyalty long after he has proven himself to be a rat. It's a bleak study of class brotherhood, shot with simplicity and acted to the highest level.

The underappreciated Treat Williams has the complex charisma of a movie star from the old studio era; he's a strong guy with an underlying river of pain. His performance is among the finest in any American film of the last twenty years, and should have won him an Oscar—or, at the very least, a lifelong dispensation against ever having to costar with Joe Piscopo.

Williams delivers all the intricacy of his character, with his wild swings between physical heroism and moral cowardice, the love he feels for the men he betrayed and his lust for the praise of those richer than he. In a subtle and nuanced performance, Williams disappears into this tortured cop.

Lumet avoids all traces of his occasionally self-conscious or overheated style. He lets the actors carry the day, and subordinates the camera work to their performances. Because the film has so many different characters and scenes, he decided to concentrate on the acting and to shoot on location as simply as possible. The reliance on location provides the gritty street feel so necessary to understanding the pressures on Williams's character.

A long, difficult, and wrenching film, with fine cop action, shoot-outs, and courtroom drama. Including stellar New York slang and amazing work from a deep supporting cast that includes Jerry Orbach (tough cop), Bob Balaban (sleazy bureaucrat), and Lindsay Crouse (cop's loyal wife). Also, some of the most inventive cursing you will ever hear.

Other recommended rentals directed by Sidney Lumet:
Dog Day Afternoon
The Hill

Q & A
Serpico
The Verdict

Putney Swope

Soul power :ATTITUDE
Anarchic, subversive 1960s comedy :MOOD

DIRECTOR: Robert Downey (1969—U.S.A.)
CAST: Arnold Johnson, Antonio Fargas, Allen Garfield
IN ENGLISH; B/W WITH SOME COLOR

Twenty-five years ago, *Putney Swope*'s wild-ass subversiveness, its willingness to tackle the taboo subjects of race and drugs, its impenetrable slang, and its frenetic air of "hipper than thou" proved sufficient to propel audiences of college-age and hippie/hipster sensibility into the theaters. Another potent marketing push may have been its presentation of a seemingly accurate black sensibility to white college boys looking to be cool. Whether those criteria suffice today should determine whether you rent this anarchic, iconic, and very funny mess. In addition to its humor, *Putney Swope* stands as its own best example of prevailing "underground" film notions of the late 1960s and is worth renting for that alone.

Robert Downey (father of the actor Robert Downey, Jr.) made three surreal, ragged comedies that were long on concept, short on structure, and budgeted on shoestrings. (The other two are *Pound* and *Greaser's Palace*) *Putney* came first and features more traditional punch lines than the others, which rely more on Downey's sense of the absurd than on what might normally be considered "jokes." Though Downey's pacing can be maddening, his schoolboy Grand Guignol is loads of fun for those whose humor inclines in that direction. If you enjoy(ed) both *Firesign Theater* and *The Three Stooges*, then perhaps Downey is for you.

"Putney Swope" is the token black man serving on the board of a Madison Avenue advertising agency. When the founder dies of a heart attack at a board meeting—which features Mel Brooks and character actor Allen Garfield—the board members immediately steal the dead man's watch and empty his pockets. They then turn to the task of electing a new chairman; they choose Putney. He evicts the entrenched power structure, changes the name of the agency to "Truth and Soul," and commissions what remain the funniest advertising parodies ever seen. A rebellion in the agency—led by *Starsky and Hutch*'s Antonio Fargas as "A-rab"—protests Putney's lifestyle, which becomes increasingly similar to that of the old boss. When the revolt turns threatening, Putney takes the money and runs, leaving the troops to sort out their own future.

The acting, like the language, camera work, and direction, is crude. Given the homemade performances and pseudo-arty, handheld cinematography, Downey's role seems closer to ringmaster than director. But that, too, is in keeping with the spirit of the times, when crazy guys found just enough money to get their deranged visions onto the screen. As a result, certain stretches are dull, others make no sense at all, and Downey's humor sinks from crude to stupid.

Maybe *Putney*'s appeal lies in the ad parodies, the fast-as-lightning (and often unintelligible) repartee, the irrepressible "underground" spirit, and the unforgettable punch lines. College campuses once rang with the sound of stoned freshmen shouting out memorable lines like: "Putney says the Borman Six girl is got to have soul!"

Or, depending on your sensibilities, maybe not.

Other recommended rentals directed by Robert Downey:
Greaser's Palace

Rancho Deluxe

Irony-fest in the modern West :**ATTITUDE**
Smart, quirky comedy :**MOOD**

DIRECTOR: Frank Perry (1974—U.S.A.)
CAST: Jeff Bridges, Sam Waterston, Slim Pickens, Elizabeth Ashley, Harry Dean Stanton
IN ENGLISH; COLOR

Charlene Dallas, Harry Dean Stanton, Slim Pickens, Richard Bright, Elizabeth Ashley, and Clifton James in *Rancho Deluxe*

The truest, funniest tale of the modern West ever told. *Rancho Deluxe* was written by Thomas McGuane (*92 in the Shade*, see page 113) and set in Livingston, Montana, once McGuane's home and now a trendy movie-star vacation paradise. Even as McGuane deplores the exploitation of the West, he furthers it by making both the landscape and the lifestyle so appealing.

Jeff Bridges and Sam Waterston star as a pair of disaffected cut-ups who turn to cattle-rustling as a cure for ennui. Slim Pickens, Elizabeth Ashley, Richard Bright, Patti D'Arbanville, and Harry Dean Stanton (way before you ever heard of him) costar. Clifton James plays the county's biggest rancher, and the man from whom the boys steal. Slim Pickens is the detective the rancher hires to chase the boys. That's the entire plot skeleton on which are hung constant, subtle gags based on McGuane's startling dialogue, a little unobtrusive slapstick, and no shortage of amusing, if occasionally adolescent, sex play. Director Frank Perry (*Diary of a Mad Housewife*) treats his players like cattle on a drive; he keeps them moving in the same direction but makes no attempts at control.

Gathering these riotous personalities in one place so far from civilization apparently let the party genie out of the bottle, resulting in anarchy on the set. The story goes that one actress had to have her big scene—a tearful LSD soliloquy—cut from the film. Seems she was too high on LSD to perform. The film echoes this sense of wild fun undercut by wanton self-destruction; if it occasionally veers into sentiment or silliness, McGuane's chiseled dialogue steers the story back on course. Harry Dean Stanton is hilarious; McGuane wrote him the goofball role of a lifetime.

McGuane absolutely nails the wide-open-spaces-yet-enclosed-lives contradiction of the modern West, and the rather desperate sense of fun those stuck in the West fall prey to. Everyone invents their own warped mythology, from the blundering ranch hands to Slim Pickens's decrepit old detective to the rich ranch-wife, who stares out of her ranch-mansion picture windows at the breathtaking white-topped mountains, and says wistfully: "Gee, I miss Schenectady sometimes."

Finally available on video, it's a longtime cult favorite, the kind of witty, well-written, evocative picture that would never get produced these days and for good reason: It didn't make a dime. Brilliant one-liners you'll remember for years and charming performances from all concerned, especially Slim Pickens and Harry Dean Stanton.

Other recommended rentals directed by Frank Perry:
Diary of a Mad Housewife

Red River

Freudian giddy-up :**ATTITUDE**
Black-and-white, rollicking, epic horse opera :**MOOD**

DIRECTOR: Howard Hawks (1948—U.S.A.)
CAST: John Wayne, Montgomery Clift, Walter Brennan, John Ireland
IN ENGLISH; B/W

Red River was the smash hit of its time. Remarkably, at that time mass entertainment could encompass themes and characters of great complexity. *Red River*'s combination of classic western action (cattle drives, stampedes, Indian attacks, shoot-outs, and hokey frontier romance) and underlying profundity (the struggle between John Wayne and Montgomery Clift) is unparalleled.

The relationship between John Wayne's "Dunston" and Montgomery Clift's "Matt" is remarkably multilayered. The two men battle on a number of thematic fronts: father versus son, rigidity versus flexibility, strength versus sensitivity, masculinity versus femininity, and totalitarianism versus democracy. Each loves the other, but each loves his own freedom more; neither will give way regardless of the consequences.

Credit the screenplay cowritten by director Hawks, which features other recurring Hawksian themes: the need for men to prove themselves to their community (here represented by the working cowboys on the cattle drive) and Hawks's insistence that moral courage stems from physical courage and that a man cannot have one without the other. Compared to most western directors, Hawks endorses a remarkable range of moral courage. He admires both Dunston's stubborn belief in his own correctness and Matt's willingness to listen to the views of others, Dunston's instant recourse to violence and Matt's reluctance to rely on gunplay.

Hawks proves less willing to grant his background characters the same complexity of motivation as Dunston or Matt. This results in inexcusable simplemindedness in the presentation of relationships between men and women, in certain action sequences, and in the interaction of minor characters. While Hawks's presentation of his women characters seems corny and dated, his treatment of Joanne Dru's character might be explained by the story that she rebuffed his attentions for her future husband, John Ireland. Ireland's role also seems weirdly truncated.

For Wayne, playing "Dunston" proved a departure, but, ironically, not a breakthrough. Never had Wayne played a character so unlovable, never had he showed such unyielding harshness. This is his finest performance, but it would hamstring him for the rest of his career. Wayne would henceforth play only unyielding macho men. His lack of compromise, sensitivity, or ability to act on his intuition when it contradicted his pride became the role model for male behavior for a generation.

For Clift, this was only his second film and his first starring role. Clift embodied the tortured actor, the sensitive genius whose sensitivity makes the world too brutal to bear. If current biographies are to be believed, Clift was a bisexual who disliked himself intensely for his sexual attraction to men. Yet the core of his brilliant, understated performance is his willingness to bare his open, compassionate, feminine side.

The contrast between Clift's uncertainty in matters of violence, sexuality, and authority, and Wayne's absolute conviction in the same arenas, elevate *Red River* beyond standard western fare. Their interplay can be seen as the inspiration for other feuding western partners whose two halves need the other for completion, such as Augustus McCrae and Captain Call in *Lonesome Dove*.

Add to this Hawks's rapid-fire dialogue, awe-inspiring wide-screen composition, a classic ensemble of 1940 character actors, and the result is the perfect rental western. There's shoot-outs for the boys, Montgomery Clift for the girls, nonstop cowboy action if you don't feel like paying attention, and brilliant psychological interplay if you do.

Other recommended rentals directed by Howard Hawks:
The Big Sleep
Bringing Up Baby
Only Angels Have Wings

Recommended traditional westerns:
My Darling Clementine (see page 109)
The Seven Samurai (directed by Akira Kurosawa)
Tom Horn (see page 173)

Robin and Marian

Adult legend :ATTITUDE
Swashbuckling love and adventure :MOOD

DIRECTOR: Richard Lester (1976—U.S.A.)
CAST: Sean Connery, Audrey Hepburn, Nicol Williamson, Robert Shaw
IN ENGLISH; COLOR

Whatever happened to Robin Hood?

Only the English could take a favorite character from myth and legend, imagine him in middle age, and follow his return to the land and glories of his youth. Then, write the characters with depth and great affection, never settle for a cheap or superficial resolution to any scene, make the costumes, settings, politics, and battles historically accurate, and join it all together with a saga of enduring love. And ensure that Richard Lester directs with his mature, mischievous knack for low-key performances, gentle sentimentality, and a classicist's sense of color.

Sean Connery and Audrey Hepburn in *Robin and Marian*

Robin Hood (Sean Connery in his finest performance) returns to England after years abroad in the Crusades. King Richard (Richard Harris in a masterful turn) dies, leaving Robin for the first time in his life with neither mission nor royal protection. Robin returns to Sherwood and discovers to his horror that Maid Marian (Audrey Hepburn, radiant and tough in a self-conscious coda to her career) has become not only a nun, but an Abbess. The Sheriff of Nottingham (Robert Shaw, self-aware, ruthless but never cruel) seeks to arrest her. Robin comes to Marian's aid and they fall in love once more. As you, Marian, Robin, and the Sheriff know it must, Robin's homecoming brings an inevitable showdown with authority.

Richard Lester brings his acute sense of history to every scene. Never drawing attention to his wealth of accurate detail, Lester lets the housing, clothes, food, methods of fighting, and courtly manners stay in the background. Living history infiltrates his tale, but serves only as the setting. Lester is careful to never put the frosting before the cake. And with stars like this, why should he?

Connery and Hepburn deliver compound thrills, primarily from their happy, confident awareness of themselves as stars working together on memorable roles and a worthy script. Their delight in one another and in their characters infuses the film with a lighthearted enthusiasm that the other actors seem to share. British Shakespearean actor Nicol Williamson's dim-witted Little John provides the perfect foil for Robin's boyish exuberance.

While Lester presents Robin as the embodiment of youthful heroism refusing to age, Marian sees Robin as the essence of manly virtues: loyalty, courage, and strength. But she fears his refusal to look into the future and imagine a day when his strength might fail him. After missing him for so long, she cannot bear to see him taken from her again. It's a complex and dark reckoning of adult love; both want to be together, but one sees only consequences and the other refuses to see any.

They don't talk like mythical figures, but as frank adults, and as usual, the woman is far more blunt than the man. While there's no shortage of sword-fights, jousting, grand-scale battles, and archery stunts, the core of the film is their loving relationship.

A great date movie, a women's movie for guys, and an action film for girls. Knowing, funny, quietly astonishing, and very moving.

Other recommended rentals directed by Richard Lester:
A Hard Day's Night
Help!
Juggernaut (see page 76)
The Three Musketeers (1974)

Rockers

"Whop'n 'Orsemout'?" :**ATTITUDE**
Lovable Rastafarian reggae fable :**MOOD**

DIRECTOR: Theodoros Bafaloukos (1979—U.S.A./Jamaica)
CAST: Winston Rodney, Leroy Wallace, Gregory Isaacs
IN ENGLISH WITH SOME SUBTITLES; COLOR

Perhaps the only film in cinema history to feature a hero named Horsemouth.

Director Bafaloukos takes a lighthearted approach to this Rasta tale, and indeed, what choice did he have? His actors are the cream of reggae musicians; in their land they walk the earth as gods. Was Bafaloukos going to show up in Trenchtown and order them about? What the musicians-turned-actors lack in thespic depth they make up for with uncontrived emotion and the charisma of unshakable self-possession.

The plot is simple and upbeat, with plenty of time for singing as waves crash against the shore (Winston Rodney of Burning Spear doing lovely a cappella), riding around Kingstown on dilapidated motorscooters painted in Ethiopian theme colors, performing onstage in reggae clubs (Horsemouth drums all around the beat, never missing it, but never hitting it directly, either), toking on spliffs the size of bowling pins, and speaking in a lilting, incomprehensible Rasta patois, for which the producers thoughtfully provide subtitles.

Horsemouth plays a reggae drummer who supports himself as a ganja delivery man. When mobsters try to horn in, Horsemouth and his pals stage a ganja strike, which foments predictable community unrest. The key to thwarting the mob lies in an inspirational combination of brotherly action and timely music. When the Rockers strike back, they imitate Robin Hood. This allows them to take vengeance on the mob, and permits Bafaloukos to indulge in Godardian commentary on insatiable consumerism.

There's a lunatics-taking-over-the-asylum feel to the whole project, a feel-good portrait of reggae street culture that performs the double duty of making its participants appear as stars but not sellouts. While bearing in mind the home-folks, *Rockers* is a deliberate outreach to an audience far beyond Jamaica, an attempt to garner commercial success on a par with the seminal, downbeat, and insightful *The Harder They Come*. Happily, *Rockers* is none of those; *Rockers* is fun.

For such a live-action cartoon, Bafaloukos provides a mature level of social realism. Even *The Harder They Come* fails to convey day-to-day shantytown life with such heart and accuracy. In his offhand but illuminating way, Bafaloukos captures the intense spiritual connection to music and marijuana that lies at the heart of the Rastafarian experience. In one amazing sequence, Horsemouth—referred to by one and all as " 'Orsemout' "—goes deep into the mountains to commune with a family of jungle-dwelling Rastas who represent a possible alternative source of ganja. The family's evident love, religious faith, self-sufficiency, and musical talent provide the least ironic, most heartfelt scenes in the film.

The sound track produced several reggae hits, including "Rockers" by Bunny Wailer and "Stepping Razor" by Sly and Robbie, which is played as a rallying cry as the entire shantytown community comes together to support Horsemouth and his gang. Older classics include "Police and Thieves" by Junior Murvin and "Book of Rules" by the Heptones.

An enjoyable jaunt through reggae country: striking tropical colors, personal appearances by top reggae stars, entertaining violence, a documentary look at shantytown life, and not a single lame song on the sound track. Lively, winsome, and well-intentioned.

Other recommended films on the reggae experience:
The Harder They Come (directed by Perry Henzell)

Rude Boy

London calling :**ATTITUDE**
Docudrama of the English Punk revolution :**MOOD**

DIRECTORS: Jack Hazan, David Mingay (1980—U.K.)
CAST: Ray Gange, Joe Strummer, Mick Jones
IN ENGLISH; COLOR

If you spent hours arguing the significance of the Clash versus the Sex Pistols, this is the film for you. If you don't know the lyrics to at least one Ramones song, don't bother. . . .

Directors Hazan and Mingay film Ray Gange, a young London punk and fanatical Clash fan, performing his own life. Ray plays himself drinking beer, cashing a dole check, shooting pool, drinking beer, making out with his girlfriend, and slowly working his way into the Clash's inner circle while drinking beer.

In Gange the directors found the epitome of the London Punk experience in all its aimlessness, contradiction, and yearned-for salvation. The Clash cooperated with, fought tooth and nail with, and then again cooperated with the filmmakers. So, the main attraction is not Ray, nor even the Clash concerts (which the band insisted on overdubbing). The most compelling moments are those spent hanging with the Clash, eavesdropping on their rehearsals, their squabbles, and most strikingly, their absolute and unhesitating morality, which Ray cannot match emotionally or politically.

If Ray could be said to have any politics, they're reflexively rightist—his racism is practically Fascist/National Front—yet the sense of identity he derives from the Clash, and from the punk alternative universe, makes him a de facto cultural leftist. Ray never tries to suss out the different urges that rule him. His rage, frustration, and refusal to find a constructive solution to either mark him as a pure, pissed-off punk. He can't even perform his duties as a Clash roadie—the achieving of which comprised his life's goal. His fuzzy political thinking and drunken incompetence make him an object of ridicule and lead to an irrevocable blowout with his idols.

Lead singer Joe Strummer is particularly hard on Ray, and shows no patience for his lack of commitment. Strummer's clearheaded intransigence in pursuit of artistic transcendence forms the other side of the Punk coin: Those like Ray remained sullen fans, those like Joe formed bands.

Strummer emerges as the film's star, a normal Joe of breathtaking charisma, iron-hard judgment, and steadfast common sense. The best music in the picture, in fact one of the best Clash songs ever (which can be heard nowhere else), is played by Strummer, alone, at a rickety piano in an old warehouse where the Clash rehearse.

Mingay and Hazan shoot with attention to color and emotional nuance, not plot or narrative. They come from the world of documentary, and have no training in drama. As a result, their pacing is mighty leisurely. But, if their pacing sucks, their timing can't be beat: They captured legendary punk-derived riots, legendary punk shows that preceded punk riots, and the Clash during their most productive period.

Other recommended rentals directed by Jack Hazan and David Mingay:
A Bigger Splash

Rumble Fish

Mythical teendom :**ATTITUDE**
Arty black-and-white coming-of-age drama :**MOOD**

DIRECTOR: Francis Ford Coppola (1983—U.S.A.)
CAST: Matt Dillon, Diane Lane, Mickey Rourke, Dennis Hopper
IN ENGLISH; B/W

Steve Smith, Matt Dillon, and Mickey Rourke in *Rumble Fish*

Coppola said he wanted to make "Camus for teenagers" and he succeeded wildly. It's shot in overheated black-and-white, with camera work and composition out of a dreamscape, and romantic violence out of some unholy merger of *West Side Story* and *Raging Bull*.

Smoke drifts over the action, and clouds are everywhere: reflected in shop windows, racing overhead, clouds to symbolize the onrushing end of innocence that has all the local teens so desperate, so violent, so determined to create their own mythology before it's too late. The feel is of an art movie made for an audience who seldom sees art films, but whose emotions are as ornate as Chinese opera: teenagers.

Matt Dillon plays Rusty James, the leader of the pack. His older brother, Motorcycle Boy, is played as the essence of outrider cool by Mickey Rourke long before his performances became a joke, back when

Rourke seemed to be the future of movie stardom. Rourke returns unexpectedly and triggers all of Rusty James's confused ideas about postteendom (which he may not live to see) and coolness (to which he aspires in Motorcycle Boy mode). Since this is a coming-of-age drama, however romantic, Rusty James must come of age, and to do so he must shed his most cherished illusions. Hence the romance, the violence, the bittersweet comedy, and the considerable emotional power of the story.

Coppola, fresh off the disastrous *One from the Heart*, exiled himself to Tulsa, Oklahoma, where he shot two films sequentially for very little money, both adaptations of S. E. Hinton novels, *Rumble Fish* and *The Outsiders* (see page 119). Working with an unusual reliance on his instincts, Coppola brought out the best in his dream cast: Dillon, Rourke, Hopper, Diane Lane, Nicolas Cage, Christopher Penn, Larry Fishburne, and singer Tom Waits.

Most of the film occurs in mythical superclose-ups or wide-angle black-and-white that alters constantly to suit the mood. Some scenes are shot in supercontrasted, hard-edged light, some in washed-out gray. The expressionist camera moves constantly, signaling the tortured emotions of the melodramatic teens. Every composition carries a significant message regarding the emotional content of the scene. Dillon has never equaled his work here; and the film's centerpiece is a long, heartbreaking chat between Dillon, Rourke, and Dennis Hopper, who plays their down-and-out dad.

As always, Hopper brings a suicidal openness to his portrayal of loss and pain. While it borders on self-parody to cast Hopper as a skid-row drunk at this juncture in his career, Hopper eats that sort of irony for breakfast. Self-abusing he may well have been, but he's still America's finest screen actor, and he found apparent redemption in this performance.

Far and away the finest film of 1983: a visual style like none other, a driving sound track by Police drummer Stewart Copeland, superb acting by Dillon, Rourke, Hopper, Lane, Penn, and Fishburne. It works as a date movie, succeeds as an art film, and stands proudly as Coppola's finest work since *Apocalypse Now*. There's nothing else like it.

Other recommended rentals directed by Francis Ford Coppola:
Apocalypse Now
The Conversation

The Godfather Parts I and II
The Outsiders (see page 119)

The Sacrifice

Russian art movie (in Swedish) **:ATTITUDE**
Exquisite, dreamlike spirituality **:MOOD**

DIRECTOR: Andrei Tarkovsky (1986—Sweden/France)
CAST: Erland Josephson, Valerie Mairesse, Susan Fleetwood
IN SWEDISH WITH ENGLISH SUBTITLES; COLOR

As if Tarkovsky didn't already make the slowest movies in the world, here he directs Swedish actors (Ingmar Bergman's everyman, Erland Josephson) speaking Swedish—the world's most sleep-inducing tongue to this English speaker—and shoots everything in shadows. Keep caffeine near to hand; although among the most meaningful achievements in cinema, few are so soporific. Renting *The Sacrifice* is not a casual decision, it's a commitment. Patience is required, and a willingness to open yourself to the process.

Tarkovsky, the supreme filmic artist of the metaphysical unknowable, here creates as profound a meditation on faith and superstition, and the bargains both demand, as Bergman ever attempted. It's beautiful, miraculous, and almost indescribably slow.

No spiritual riddle comes already solved, and Tarkovsky was determined that his viewers should seek with the same intensity as he. Just when an apparent clue appears, the screen darkens, and one peers into a murky mix of browns and shadows, convinced that the answer lurks somewhere within. And all the while the camera moves dreamily, in tracking shots that become pans, close-ups that metamorphosize into zoom-outs, and still frames composed like the paintings of Vermeer.

Erland Josephson (*Scenes from a Marriage*) plays a scholarly director living in self-imposed exile in the lovely north-country lakelands with his unfaithful, high-strung wife, his dependent daughter, and the men who circle around them. He finds his world, and himself, worthy only of contempt, and masks his despair with irony and intellectual pronouncements. He scoffs at religion as he scoffs at life and loves only his young son.

Into the midst of his hopelessness comes a hint, just the tiniest hint, that the world is about to be destroyed by nuclear holocaust. (None of this is spelled out, so if you don't want the Cliffs Notes, if you want to discover these mysteries for yourself, skip this paragraph.) Erland communes with an apparent witch and promises to sacrifice everything if the miserable normal order of the world is restored.

It is restored, and he does sacrifice all, in an apocalyptic conflagration that must be the envy of all cinematic apocalyptic conflagration experts—Peckinpah, Tarantino, and Antonioni included. Was it all a dream? Is his sacrifice simple vanity or the essence of prayer? Is anyone watching at home still awake?

No other director has Tarkovsky's eye for color in the natural world: the green of grass and trees, the brown of floors and furniture, the grays of sea and sky, the screaming yellows of flame. No one could invest the presentation of these colors, or the photographing of their sources in the world, with such poetry.

Tarkovsky moves his camera like no one else. He captures the unreal movement, heightened reality, and fractured time of dreaming as no one else can. He directs his actors in a languid form of speech and movement that intensifies the dreamlike spell his images cast. Tarkovsky presents the metaphysical, the spiritual, the unconscious, and the emotional with startling directness.

The Sacrifice broods, it confounds, it illuminates, it raises up, and it casts down; it answers its own questions with riddles—riddles that serve as metaphors of sight, sound, and movement that can only be expressed in cinema. And while each image is more wondrous than the one preceding, all serve the story, and the story serves Tarkovsky's quest. His quest is knowledge, which leads, as it must, to only greater mystery.

Other recommended rentals directed by Andrei Tarkovsky:

Alexander Rubelev

Nostalgia

Stalker (see page 158)

The Sheltering Sky

Existential travelogue avec doomed love :ATTITUDE
Magnificent, depressive art movie :MOOD

DIRECTOR: Bernardo Bertolucci (1990—U.S.A.)
CAST: Debra Winger, John Malkovich, Campbell Scott, Paul Bowles
IN ENGLISH; COLOR

Bernardo Bertolucci adapted this seminal hipster/beat novel by Paul Bowles, which traces the doomed journey of an American expatriate couple—on the run from a soul-destroying bourgeois life and their own ennui—lost in the wilds of the northern Sahara. John Malkovich and Debra Winger (and, indeed, the entire cast and crew) travel into the least accessible, most desolate reaches of North Africa. The farther into the wilderness they go, the farther their souls recede. Their desperate search for connection—to one another, to their own sensations, to the mysterious world around them—only leads to increasingly mortal peril.

And the more remote their location, the more spectacular the camera work becomes. Cinematographer Vittorio Storraro (*Apocalypse Now*) reveals this alien land in complex lyrical swoops or close-ups lit like Rembrandt portraits. The camera choreography that Bertolucci and Storraro achieve in the middle of nowhere—far from any technical, logistical, financial, medical, or emotional assistance—reflects their absolute devotion to the illuminated image. Bertolucci seems more emotionally connected to these characters than any in his oeuvre, probably because he and his crew share the odyssey his characters undertake.

Malkovich and Winger play a couple adrift, mutual alienation binds them more closely than love. They share the saddest, truest sex scene ever filmed. . . . It's familiar territory for Bertolucci, which he explores with more delicacy than usual; perhaps his respect for the source material led him to simply interpret events as presented by Bowles, rather than rewrite them. It's tough to separate Winger's own behavior from that of her character, but she appears convincingly lost. Bertolucci's adaptation grants the male characters, played by John Malkovich and Campbell Scott, more depth, but that's an accurate reflection of the book.

While the camera movement seems designed to illuminate character, it also provides constant proof of Bertolucci's determination to do his best work no matter how difficult the circumstances. As Winger moves across Africa in a camel caravan, there's little dialogue and none of it in English. But Storraro's images command attention and each image is more lovely than the last. The plot moves slowly, and each plot payoff brings only increasing tragedy, yet the poetry of the images somehow promise redemption.

One of the most rewarding and least appreciated films of the last few years. Oblique, arty, and not for the faint of heart.

Other recommended rentals directed by Bernardo Bertolucci:
The Conformist (see page 31)
The Last Emperor
Last Tango in Paris

Sorcerer/Wages of Fear
Existential joyride, Parts I & II :**ATTITUDE**
No-nonsense manly thriller :**MOOD**

Sorcerer

DIRECTOR: William Friedkin (1977—U.S.A.)
CAST: Roy Scheider, Bruno Crémer, Francesco Rabal, Soudad Amidou
IN ENGLISH; COLOR

Sorcerer

Wages of Fear

DIRECTOR: H.G. Clouzot (1948—France)
CAST: Yves Montand, Vera Clouzot, Charles Vanel
IN FRENCH WITH ENGLISH SUBTITLES; B/W

It's a suspense and adventure classic, first told by French director H.G. Clouzot as *The Wages of Fear*. *Sorcerer* is the American remake.

The plot of both films is the same and it's darn simple: Four men on the lam with nothing to lose drive two trucks filled with nitroglycerin over a nightmare mountain road in the most isolated country on earth. If they blow up—so what? Their lives weren't worth much anyway. If they make it—enough money for total redemption.

The essential existential stuff: do things right, be brave, and triumph. Provided, of course, that fate and coincidence don't make a mockery of all your efforts. And provided that you don't get what your corrupt soul really deserves no matter how brave you pretend to be.

Fresh off his triumph of *The Exorcist*, William Friedkin laid his money and credibility on the line to make the very first bloated Hollywood thriller—*Sorcerer* cost $22 million to make in 1976! Unlike most arrogant, self-indulgent Hollywood guys, however, Friedkin put every dime onto the screen. It fairly glistens, lit with piercing, glowing blues under an action-movie sheen of diamond-hard white light.

Roy Scheider stars as a low-life Boston hoodlum on the run. His fellow fugitives—a Frenchman, an Arab, and a Latin American hit man—live in an uneasy community of expatriates in the most appalling vision of a South American backwater ever created for film. In fact, the worst aspects of it don't seem created at all; they appear all too real. Somewhere in this miserable country, terrorists have blown up an oil well. Scheider's mission—and he has no choice but to accept it—is to drive with three companions across mountains, rivers, swamps, and deserts. Their trucks are unreliable, slow, and packed with explosives so cranky they might be set off by a vigorous sneeze.

Friedkin, who shot in eight different countries, creates a detailed back-story for each fugitive, so the film begins—with no explanation—by jumping from one character's prologue to the next. No apparent connection exists until Scheider wakes up in hell, and he meets those who screwed up as badly as he, those who ran until they could run no farther.

Now they want redemption, meaning a return to the world, and they will do anything to get it. And that's the whole of the plot: First you meet the guys—which takes the first half of the film—then they drive the trucks, which takes the second half. Pure adrenaline with an economy of expression; not one wasted moment from start to finish.

Wages of Fear, the original version, is longer, meaner in spirit, slightly cruder in cinema, features more harrowing stunts, and suffers from 1940s sexism and costumes. It's also French, which means that the lash of fate is both crueler and funnier. If the roads Yves Montand and his three compatriots drive over are not quite so terrifying as those in *Sorcerer,* the suspense is greater. Nothing is faked; those ancient trucks appear to be hovering on the brink every second. . . .

With his single lens, unmoving camera, and apparent determination to kill his cast, Clouzot merges the (basically Hollywood) prewar action extravaganza (*The Four Feathers*) with the (basically European) postwar personal-statement picture. In keeping with prevailing European trends—meaning no one had any money—Clouzot shoots mostly outdoors in a simple visual style. His function-over-form approach stands up fifty years later; the spare, elegant frames grant the stunts/suspense center stage. The most harrowing physical and emotional carnage is shot in long unbroken takes, and the agony on his actors' faces cannot be entirely make-believe. Without such a restrained style, the unceasing tension might be lurid or even stupid. With it, Clouzot achieves a classic.

Try not to let the extremely dated opening wreck *Wages of Fear*'s credibility. Due to the aforementioned 1940s sexism, women may find that difficult, but the thrills of the remaining two hours reward endurance handsomely. Though both films share a story line, they are so different, and so compelling on their own terms, that both should be seen, though I recommend viewing on separate nights.

Suspense? Rent either of these and claw all the upholstery off the arms of your chair.

Other recommended rentals directed by William Friedkin:
The Exorcist
The French Connection
To Live and Die in L.A.

Other recommended rentals directed by H.G. Clouzot:
Diabolique (1955)

The Spy Who Came in from the Cold

Cold War downer :**ATTITUDE**
Unsentimental, intelligent spy story :**MOOD**

DIRECTOR: Martin Ritt (1965—U.K.)
CAST: Richard Burton, Claire Bloom, Oskar Werner
IN ENGLISH; B/W

Richard Burton describes his character as one of the "seedy, squalid little men," and this picture wallows in the unrelieved seediness he describes. Director Martin Ritt (*Hombre;* see page 63) sticks like glue to John Le Carré's pessimistic novel of the cynical understanding between the men who performed espionage dirty work on either side of the Iron Curtain.

Burton plays a low-end British spy ordered to defect. As he drinks and gets into fights—the better to create the image of a cast-out degenerate and thereby become more appealing bait to the Soviets—he falls in love with the ethereal Claire Bloom, who plays a naive member of the British Communist Party. Once taken by the Russians, Burton finds himself on trial in East Berlin as he participates in the court-martial of an East German agent whom Burton "defected" in order to destroy. Only a connoisseur of lies about lies could untangle the game that follows, and Burton is more than equal to the task. What he cannot but must do is connect to his own emotions. Burton played noisier film roles (*Who's Afraid of Virginia Woolf?*) and he played more melodramatically tortured souls (*Night of the Iguana*), but he was never more cunning or acute, never more fully vested in a character, and never so controlled.

Director Martin Ritt is no visual stylist; he frames the action simply and lets it happen. Ritt obtains fine, quiet performances from his predominantly English cast, something few American directors have accomplished. The violence is mostly verbal, and the actors deliver their spoken bullets in tellingly sedate tones. They know the power their words carry; they don't have to shout. By his omission of any James Bond–style car chases or explosions, author Le Carré identifies such stuff as claptrap. He makes this pressurized, traitorous world seem quite real, and perhaps it is.

There's little music, and the silences behind the dialogue differ in each locale, from shabby coffee shop to cheesy strip club to oppressive courtroom. Each silence has its own ambience, and all are malevolent.

(It's interesting that Ritt should do his best work with a Le Carré novel. George Roy Hill achieved uncharacteristic subtlety with his little-seen but worthy adaptation of another Le Carré novel, *The Little Drummer Girl,* in which Diane Keaton gives her finest non–Woody Allen performance.)

The movie does not try to pretty up—and thereby ruin—the grim intent of a less-than-sunny book. The film's commitment to an unredeemed acceptance of Burton's sordid predicament turns this unhappy tale into an illuminating tragedy, while also providing a study of realpolitik, character, middle-aged love, and the redemption of genuine sacrifice.

Other recommended rentals directed by Martin Ritt:
Hombre (see page 63)

Stalker

Russian art movie (in Russian) :**ATTITUDE**
Enrapturing spiritual quest :**MOOD**

DIRECTOR: Andrei Tarkovsky (1979—U.S.S.R.)
CAST: Aleksandr Kaidanovsky, Anatoly Solonitsin
IN RUSSIAN WITH ENGLISH SUBTITLES; COLOR AND B/W

An unbelievably slow meditation on the necessary difficulty of any quest for spirituality, and the limited potential for man's redemption. *Stalker* is shot in endlessly long, uninterrupted takes, and fueled by nonstop Russian rumination on the Really Big Questions.

Unlike Bergman, who approached the cosmic verities via a stern Scandinavian intellect, Tarkovsky seems a natural mystic. His films have a distinctive look, pace, and purpose, born of his unmediated presentation of the metaphysical world through the normally unwieldy tool of cinema. Tarkovsky's reality-shattering special effects—and certain camera movements—seem hardly possible in a Newtonian universe, but there they are. Since he's both a mystic and a magician, Tarkovsky's films are not diversions, but explorations.

In an oppressive police state, in the heart of a ruined city, lives a man who leads others into a forbidden region that lies outside the city walls, sealed by armed guards and barbed wire. That region is the Zone, and that man is the Stalker. The Stalker guides a cynical, verbose writer (representing the Artist) and a stubborn, mumbling professor (representing Empiricism). The writer and the professor seek the Room at the center of the Zone. The Room has the power to fulfill their deepest wishes, or so says the legend of the Zone.

They face machine-gun fire, steal a railroad car, and make their way into the Zone. Once there, the film shifts from eerie sepia tones to the washed-out colors of hallucination. As they move through the haunting landscape, the Stalker describes the dangers of the Zone: Any place that was safe on a previous visit is fatal today; one must always leave by a different route than one entered; and one never travels in a straight line. The three set off, through tunnels, puddles, green fields, and industrial waste. Water is everywhere; they slog through streams, lie down in filthy pools, wash in ponds, and rest by rivers.

The Stalker's success depends on his ability to psychically intuit the shifting moods of the Zone and to guide his clients accordingly. The amorphous, deadly nature of the place is belied by its pastoral appearance, and the pilgrims are more willing to believe their eyes than their guide. Each rebels against the Stalker's wisdom. Each tries to go his own way. Can they survive the trek? Can they find the Room? Will their wishes be granted?

Though Tarkovsky draws unbearable tension from these questions, he regards them as secondary. His interest lies in the quest and he understands quests to be drawn-out affairs, each with its own discipline. Tarkovsky elongates every moment, and to watch is to experience time slowing down with an accompanying sense of enveloping meditation. After the rapid-fire, synapse-slicing of MTV, it may take a while to grow accustomed to Tarkovsky's stately awareness of the flow of every single second. However restless the first ten minutes make you, try not to struggle; accepting and embracing induces a lingering sense of rapturous wonder.

While *The Sacrifice* is like a dream, *Stalker* more closely resembles the visual language and logical/illogical structure of a drug-induced experience. By conventional standards, little happens, but each moment seems profoundly weighted. As the characters speak, we seem to be able to see into their souls. When the camera moves, we follow every nuance, searching for the underlying meaning that Tarkovsky finds in this world of weird colors, underground tunnels, sinister black dogs, and rusty swinging doors. There is no more explaining his method than there is resisting it.

Years after viewing, you may not remember the plot, but you will recall the sound of water—trickling streams, quiet pools, loud splashes, gurgling rapids, and ominous drips—all part of the sonic poetry of Tarkovsky's philosophical landscape.

Other recommended rentals directed by Andrei Tarkovsky:

Alexander Rubolev

Nostalgia

The Sacrifice (see page 151)

State of Things

Art movie meets B-thriller **:ATTITUDE**
Meditative film within a film **:MOOD**

DIRECTOR: Wim Wenders (1982—U.S.A.)
CAST: Sam Fuller, Alan Gorwitz, Viva
IN ENGLISH AND SOME GERMAN WITH ENGLISH SUBTITLES; B/W

Fleeing the corporate hell that directing and editing his Hollywood debut (*Hammett*) had become, Wenders wrote and directed this bitter, beautiful tale of the unending war between creativity and commercialism that comprises the Hollywood experience. Only Wenders would make an independent art-house picture as relaxation from the stress of making a big-studio commercial movie.

State of Things marked the beginning of Wenders's collaboration with the cinematographer Henri Aliekan, who photographed the films of Jean Cocteau. Aliekan's black-and-white cinematography is less expressionist than the camera work of Wenders's better-known *Wings of Desire*. The compositions recall the still photography of Robert Frank. The visual style harkens to the low-contrast, all-gray tones of John Ford's *My Darling Clementine* (see page 109).

Gathering a cast of eccentrics (Warhol actress Viva, pulp auteur Samuel Fuller, Paul Getty, and Allen Garfield), Wenders shot half his story in Lisbon and returned to L.A. for the finale. Seminal independent/trash film producer-director Roger Corman plays a flint-hearted studio executive, and Allen Gooritz (né Garfield) should have won an Oscar for his portrayal of a failed producer on the run from the mob.

Hiding from pursuing hit men, the director and the producer cruise L.A. all night in a borrowed Winnebago. As they ride, Wenders's doppelgänger sits in silence while Gooritz's character—who was apparently modeled on Francis Ford Coppola—talks endlessly about the film business. Though an eerie, unnameable tension suffuses the entire picture, this all-night ride is as suspenseful as the finest films noir.

Wenders has seldom been as insightful, as compact, or as assured. *State of Things*, though demanding in the usual Wenders way—slow and not well explained—has a fierce, uplifting quality. There's genius in Wenders's patient building of a story, and in his deep appreciation for the beauty of the world as it appears in black-and-white.

Other recommended rentals directed by Wim Wenders:
Alice in the Cities
The American Friend (see page 4)
Paris, Texas
Wings of Desire

Straight Time

Neofuckingrealism :**ATTITUDE**
Gritty crime story :**MOOD**

DIRECTOR: Ulu Grosbard (1978—U.S.A.)
CAST: Dustin Hoffman, Gary Busey, Kathy Bates, Theresa Russell, Harry Dean Stanton
IN ENGLISH; COLOR

While serving time for armed robbery, convict Edward Bunker wrote the novel on which this movie is based. His gritty street realism and morally correct violence (from a professional criminal's perspective) attracted Dustin Hoffman, who developed this project and made it his own. Hoffman chose theater director Ulu Grosbard, who had recently directed Hoffman in the quirky and wonderful *Who Is Harry Kellerman and Why Is He Saying Those Terrible Things About Me?*

Harry Dean Stanton and Dustin Hoffman in *Straight Time*

Grosbard (*True Confessions, Georgia*) pulls together a cast of three future Oscar winners (Hoffman, Gary Busey, and Kathy Bates) and directs with his usual unadorned style, drawing extraordinary performances from his actors. He achieves a high standard of grubby reality in the costumes, dialogue, settings, and demonstrating the how-tos of armed robbery. Even the wildest crimes and most explosive bursts of violence shed light on the characters. Nothing is gratuitous; every scene links to every other. The screenplay is uncommonly well constructed and tight. It's also the first to insert the word "fucking" in the midst of other words, as in "unfuckingprofessional" or "outfuckingrageous." This gives the dialogue a sharp, realistic rhythm.

Hoffman plays a stickup man released from prison who finds a job, a girl—and that life on parole is more trying than jail. He returns to what he knows best, reuniting with his favorite partner, wonderfully played by Harry Dean Stanton, and together they go on a spree. They rob jewelry stores and banks with a professional joy founded on pure psychosis. Harry Dean robs to escape his suburban life; he's desperate for kicks. Hoffman is much scarier; his criminality springs from a primordial antisocial malfunction. When things go awry, the malfunction asserts itself. Hoffman becomes possessed by an inflexible code of convict morality that disregards all consequences in the achieving of its Old Testament justice.

The supporting cast was then mostly unknowns and reflects the low-budget/high-commitment nature of the project. Gary Busey plays Hoffman's useless junkie pal, Kathy Bates is Busey's wife, and Theresa Russell makes her screen debut as Hoffman's girlfriend. M. Emmet Walsh plays Hoffman's sleazy parole officer. Hoffman appears in every scene, subordinating himself completely to his character.

Hoffman presents a once-whole man fractured into pieces. His portrayal of a convict is a Chinese puzzle box of hidden emotions and undiscussed intents. He has a different face for everyone: tender and kind to his girlfriend; ruthless on the job or when seeking revenge; solicitous of Harry Dean; and completely shut down when in prison. Theresa Russell tries to bring him out, Harry Dean tries to calm him down, and everyone else fears him.

There's a pensive air of sadness underlying Hoffman's time with Theresa Russell, as he and we know that he cannot stay out in the world for long. Eventually he will drive himself back to the universe in which he's comfortable: the unfeeling world of prison.

A rare combination of violence with a true-crime feel, and the sort of acting seldom seen in a caper film, especially one with such well-done capers.

Other recommended rentals directed by Ulu Grosbard:

Georgia
True Confessions
Who Is Harry Kellerman and Why Is He Saying Those Terrible
Things About Me?

Suture

Deadpan cinematic in-joke :**ATTITUDE**
Lengthy, arty suspense :**MOOD**

DIRECTORS: Scott McGehee, David Siegel (1995—U.S.A.)
CAST: Dennis Hasbert, Mel Harris, Sab Shimono, Dina Merrill
IN ENGLISH; B/W

Suture was shot in old-fashioned wide-screen black-and-white. It's a murder mystery, a love story, an existential paradigm on the essential obscurity of self, and a nasty lesson on assumptions of racial identity. It's Ozu meets *The 10th Victim* meets *Blow-Up* meets *Putney Swope* (see page 138).

Two long-lost twin brothers—one rich, one poor—reunite after years of separation. The rich brother, Vincent, tries to murder the poor brother, Clay, so everyone will think that Vincent died instead. But Clay survives and is mistaken for Vincent, who's off hiding. Owing to the violence of the attempt on his life, Clay contracts that old cinematic favorite, amnesia. He can't remember who he is, though he gets glimpses of his past via disturbing flashbacks. Clay falls in love with his doctor (played by Mel Harris, from *thirtysomething*) and moves into Vincent's rich, comfortable life. Everyone around Clay tries to convince him that he's Vincent, but Clay has his doubts. Clay experiences an epiphany of recognition just as Vincent returns, pistol in hand and homicide in his heart. Who will survive?

Who survives is not the point. The point is that Vincent is played by a white actor and Clay by a black actor and no character in the movie ever notices or calls attention to the fact. Watching the plot unfold around this grand conceit triggers a number of interesting reactions—laughter, an interior study of one's own notions on race, horror, fascination, and amusement.

The filmmakers shoot in a distanced, deadpan, early-1970s European-art-movie style. They pack the foreground with close-ups set against an endless deep-focus background. It's a crisp, arresting look, evoking cheap black-and-white thrillers, and more than a few early-1960s Japanese films (which influenced early-1970s European art movies). McGehee and Siegel, for all their intellectual in-jokes, understand slow-paced thrillers. While their taste is too art-school for quick cutting, drawn-out gunplay, or car chases, there are several sequences of excruciating suspense and one amazing showdown.

Suture is more of an art film in noir's clothing than the reverse. The directors use noir conventions to present their ideas on modern culture—the urge to conform, what comprises identity, certain assumptions on race, and, most importantly, our own expectations of what a movie should explain to us. *Suture*, bless its heart, explains nothing.

Take it as funny, as nihilistic, as a thriller commenting on thrillers, as an irritating, masturbatory exercise by snot-nosed art geeks, or as a visionary work by filmmakers of genuine originality inventing their own ironic thriller/trash film–derived style. That they reject many of the best-loved narrative virtues only makes their work more rewarding. Or all the more off-putting, depending on your taste.

Its artiness may condemn it, unfairly, as a film for art snobs, for those who prefer references to narrative, and jokes that make you nod in satisfied recognition rather than laugh aloud. In other words, it's a film by and for film freaks. If you're a film freak or an art snob or have an adventurous sense of humor, enjoy.

Sweet Smell of Success

Show-biz hell **:ATTITUDE**
Mean-spirited urban drama **:MOOD**

DIRECTOR: Alexander MacKendrick (1957—U.S.A.)
CAST: Burt Lancaster, Tony Curtis, Susan Harrison
IN ENGLISH; B/W

Tony Curtis and Burt Lancaster in *Sweet Smell of Success*

Playwright Clifford Odets didn't indict society with this screenplay, he burned it to the ground. The story concerns purely American ambition and renders the components of such—ass-kissing, corruption, betrayal, doomed good deeds—in avid detail. Yet, for all of Odets's meanness of spirit, the film is no morality tract. Its characters are eagerly evil, jovial in their viciousness; their enthusiasm for their own depraved lives is never subsumed to anything so corny as a "message." Burt Lancaster plays an omnipotent gossip columnist in New York City. Lancaster's desperately ambitious, shameless assistant, played by Tony Curtis in the performance of his lifetime, will do anything to curry favor with Burt.

Lancaster holds court in a New York nightclub while Curtis scrambles around the nighttime city, wrecking reputations, lying, and wheedling, all on Burt's behalf. Lancaster assigns Curtis the odious task of derailing the current romance of Lancaster's psychologically frail younger sister. Lancaster is obsessed with keeping his sister's love to himself; he'd rather destroy her than let her become an adult. Lancaster's repressed incestuous urges seem even creepier because his character's lust is so unconscious, so masked in fatherly well meaning. In the carrying-out of Lancaster's assignment, Curtis finds himself smitten by the urge to do a good deed. If he succumbs, however, Lancaster will make him pay.

The story moves quickly. The self-revealing dialogue (Lancaster to Curtis: "You're like a cookie full of arsenic.") emerges in furtive little bursts, as everyone either whispers or shouts. Lancaster shifts from unctuous to vicious in an eyeblink. Odets parses New York's never-mentioned but iron-clad class system; he notes the tiny snubs that can shatter twenty years of social climbing.

The cinematography by American legend James Wong Howe combines Howe's typically classic composition with a gritty, on-location edge. For Howe, the dark city offers no shortage of visual metaphors. The shadow-lines that fall across Lancaster's face are sharp enough to shave with, and never have the pools of light thrown by streetlamps promised such salvation, or the inky darkness around them such despair.

This either/or world is tinged by Oedipal tragedy, as Lancaster and Curtis play out an intense father-son competition, both striving for the adoration of mom (Lancaster's sister). Odets presents these themes with a blithe straightforwardness, as if daring the censors to admit that they recognized the underlying archetypal struggles. Adding to the amorality is that Odets makes it clear that corruption allows his characters to achieve their goals of money, sex, and public recognition. For Odets, achieving these goals requires the sale of one's soul.

It's practically a Scorsese picture, with its merciless, classically derived themes, after-hours netherworld, and neorealist dialogue. As in *Casino* and *Mean Streets*, the characters move through a shabby, brutal, self-contained universe. As in Scorsese's best work, the characters are so compelling that their flaws do not lessen our interest—they sustain it.

It's a nervy piece of work: complex, adult, and spiteful.

The Tall Guy

Date movie :**ATTITUDE**
Whimsical, smart love story (with a believable happy ending) :**MOOD**

DIRECTOR: Mel Smith (1990—U.K.)
CAST: Emma Thompson, Jeff Goldblum
IN ENGLISH; COLOR

When it comes to romantic comedies, English taste is markedly different from American. In a reversal of the American formula, the English prefer their romance explicit and their comedy implied. English romantic comedies also tend to view sex as a normal aspect of adult life, and so avoid the emphasis on "scoring" that makes their American counterparts seem so juvenile.

From Richard Curtis, screenwriter of *Four Weddings and a Funeral*, comes an inexplicably neglected wonder starring Jeff Goldblum as a bumbling actor adrift in London and Emma Thompson as the nurse he pursues.

Deriving perhaps from the humane, funny—and stark-naked—sex scenes, or from the too-familiar way Goldblum makes a fool of himself in pursuit of both love *and* lust, men and women tend to enjoy this film equally. There are no dead spots, no embarrassing sappiness or insulting sexism. The characters seem all too real, from their wounded hearts to their clumsy tongues to their less-than-perfect bodies (what a relief!). Curtis's dialogue casts Goldblum as a man who can't quite say what he means, and Thompson as a woman cursed by her gift for ironic bluntness. They make a perfect couple.

Director Mel Smith debuts with this film—after a career as a comic actor—and his budgetary constraints definitely show. Happily, Smith's cinematic limitations and the film's rather homemade quality make the film more welcoming and more lovable.

Smith avoids the American style of screaming every punch line at top volume. In keeping with the English tradition of quiet irony, many of the best jokes are throwaways, and one needs to pay close attention. The occasional—and very English—lapses into silliness are redeemed by the film's final quarter, which features a fully staged parody of an Andrew Lloyd Webber musical. The plot comes to a halt so we can all enjoy the singing and dancing of . . . a musical staging of *The Elephant Man!*

Goldblum charmingly mocks himself with great style. Emma Thompson happily sacrifices her dignity—and takes off all her clothes. Brit stand-up Rowan Atkinson has a wonderful sour turn as Jeff Goldblum's nightmare of a boss.

A film for an evening of giggles, popcorn, and sincere snuggling.

Other recommended sweet, modern English comedies:
Clockwise (directed by Christopher Morahan)
Four Weddings and a Funeral (Mike Newell)
Gregory's Girl (Bill Forsyth)
The Ice Cream Wars (Bill Forsyth)
Local Hero (Bill Forsyth)

Tapeheads

Hip references run amok **:ATTITUDE**
Surreal parodies of music videos **:MOOD**

DIRECTOR: Bill Fishman (1989–U.S.A.)
CAST: John Cusack, Tim Robbins, Mary Crosby, Jello Biafra
IN ENGLISH; COLOR

A wild and intermittently hilarious conglomeration of music-industry in-jokes, hip references, and subtle physical humor provided by costars John Cusack and Tim Robbins. They play underemployed security guards who turn to making music videos. Their comedic timing and interplay suggests much hard work and even more goodwill.

To give a sense of director Bill Fishman's endlessly referential and strikingly intelligent (or unbelievably sophomoric when it suits him) sense of humor, Tim Robbins's parents are played by Doug McClure and Connie Stevens; *Soul Train*'s Don Cornelius plays a shady music producer; Sam Moore (of Sam and Dave) and Junior Walker (of "Shotgun" fame) play a faded soul act known as the Swanky Modes; and punk-rock pioneer Jello Biafra, of the Dead Kennedys, appears as an FBI agent.

It's damn strange to see a movie that parodies music videos—an art form for under-thirties if there ever was one—but offers sophisticated slapstick and pop-culture icons that only over-forties might recognize. This is perhaps one explanation for *Tapeheads*'s complete lack of box-office success. Yet neither the story nor the jokes are all that arcane, and the film's anarchic reveling in its own existence will bring a smile.

There's no arguing with Fishman's willingness to leap headfirst into pure rock surrealism. Devo frontman Mark Mothersbaugh wrote much of the music, the black rock band Fishbone appears as a country music act, and *Dallas* star Mary Crosby gives her all as a nunchuka-toting record executive on the make. Stiv Bators of the Dead Boys cameos as a cock-rocking lead singer, and Weird Al Yankovic plays the stupidest fan in rock 'n' roll history.

Fishman has yet to direct another feature; it's inspiring to see him squander his shot at the big time indulging his ambitiously fringe sense of humor. The story wends from hilarious full-length video parody to groovy jokes based on arcane knowledge of record-business trivia.

If you have fewer than five hundred CDs in your collection, many of the best jokes will pass you by, but the commitment to one man's vision, as evidenced by the performances of Robbins and Cusack, will more than make up for any missed laughs. To those who own thousands of records and are proud of it, Fishman stands revealed as a genius of cool, a man who refused to compromise his parodic principles and whose one film warrants him the status of legend. Or, to quote Tim Robbins: "Legend? Nay, *God!*"

Worship at the altar of Fishman, and come away with your faith in subversive comedy and soul music restored.

Thief

Modern noir :**ATTITUDE**
Riveting, monosyllabic caper flick :**MOOD**

DIRECTOR: Michael Mann (1981—U.S.A.)
CAST: James Caan, Tuesday Weld, James Belushi
IN ENGLISH; COLOR

Only once did Michael Mann (*The Last of the Mohicans, Heat*) put a lid on the compulsive mythmaking that makes his later work so overblown. Only once did he understate, and when he did, a classic emerged.

James Caan, playing a jewel thief—and a living, breathing, cool-guy meta-

Tom Signorelli and James Caan in *Thief*

phor for the outlaw/artist in society—makes the classic mistake of trading his freelance ways for the illusion of security. Way more security than he prefers, compliments of his new partners, the Mob. Caan discovers that having once compromised in order to join, he must be absolutely uncompromising—that is, he must kill people—to escape. The (criminal) corporate world is a nasty place and the artist in particular must be willing to defend his art.

The artist-metaphorical stuff does not dilute the Americanness of Mann's vision and nobody's more American than he. Mann loves gritty cities, tough-talking cops, and big, shiny American cars, guns, and gear. With his scheming underworld of electronic experts, metallurgists, and forgers, Mann creates an alternative universe of Horatio Algers: men who use their native cunning to fulfill their ambitions, however illegal. While wrestling with his artist's dilemma, Caan strives to create a home life with Tuesday Weld (corrupted innocence incarnate), to get his mentor, Willie Nelson (uncorrupted integrity incarnate), out of jail, and to pull off the most compelling, most gear-intensive safe-cracking (American ingenuity incarnate) in movie history.

Caan's thief is as American as can be: He distrusts language, derives his identity from his work, and has a chip on his shoulder the size of Mount Rushmore. Ditto the crime capers; they feature sexy high-tech tools and techniques, and Mann loves them. He shoots adoring close-ups of every tool, which, naturally, includes a bevy of sexy sidearms. He follows a lock-breaking device into the lock itself, zooming into a hole drilled into a safe in that rarest of moments: a shot never before attempted. It's a measure of Mann's visual inventiveness, and of his determination that every frame be compelling.

Mann tamps down the story's emotions. Everyone seems under intense pressure from within. Characters speak in oblique references, using an almost impenetrable street slang. The mood starts out claustrophobic, and gets more so as Caan's options are chipped away one by one. Something has to give, to explode. That something turns out to be Caan's notions of "the good life." His fantasies of merging freedom and security go to hell, and Caan follows them.

Caan underplays his character, and gives a fine performance. Willie Nelson's role is brief but iconic. Tuesday Weld is impossibly beautiful and remote, and James Belushi is at least competent. Mann got everyone to do their best work and in so doing, did his own.

Stylish, moody, trendy in the best possible way (a hypnotic, pulsating score from Tangerine Dream), nice explosions, guns galore, excops as character actors, and plenty of Armani—albeit circa 1980—on everybody, even the sleazy cops.

Other recommended rentals directed by Michael Mann:
The Last of the Mohicans (1992)
Manhunter

Thief of Bagdad

Technicolor dream :**ATTITUDE**
Extravagant kid's fantasy for adults :**MOOD**

DIRECTORS: Michael Powell, Ludwig Berger, Tim Whelan, Zoltan
    Korda (1940—U.K.)
CAST: Sabu, Conrad Veidt, Mary Morris
IN ENGLISH; TECHNICOLOR

Winner of Oscars for Set Design, Cinematography, and Special Effects, this lavish Technicolor fantasy has developed several parallel, contradictory identities: children's classic, camp screamer, and enduring fable for adults.

John Justin adds fuel to the campfire by his wimpy performance as a worthy Persian king duped and then blinded by an evil wizard, played with fearsome charisma by Conrad Veidt. Sabu plays the thief, on whom the wizard casts a spell. The wizard turns Sabu, for half the picture, into a yappy little dog.

Whether his form is human or canine, the thief serves as the king's protector as they race from adventure to adventure, all to save the princess, whom both the king and the wizard desire. Midway through, the story abandons the prince and princess (a pair of stiffs) to follow Sabu's journey to "the roof of the world," whence he is borne on the back of a giant genie, played by American actor Rex Ingram wearing a big red diaper and curly toenails.

There—in the terrifying centerpiece fantasy—Sabu breaks into a forbidden temple, climbs an enormous spiderweb, battles a horrible giant spider, and steals "the all-seeing eye" from the forehead of a sacred sculpture. Accomplished with little dialogue and a wealth of detail, this sequence spares no Freudian image. The deliberate use of physical forms with significant psychological potency—spiders, octopi, multiarmed women who kill—showcases the splendidly warped imagination of codirector Michael Powell.

Reviving his childhood nightmares with a courage bordering on the pathological, Powell renders images that are true to the archetypal aspect of all fairy tales: His genie is both provider and destroyer (like the overwhelming paternal authority he represents), and his thief, is overboiling with homoerotic appeal. Sabu's androgyny makes him appealing to both young girls and boys, as any children's hero(ine) must be. His mocking persona also allows Sabu to become a commentator on the plot (the imp or jester, who mocks the proceedings even as he shapes them), with its simple tale of thwarted love and blundering heroism. Sabu's character remains consistent; when offered riches, stability, and education, the thief runs away. He prefers to remain the eternal child.

The colors—a key aspect of the narrative—are rich and lurid beyond any in modern films, thanks to the three-strip Technicolor process, and the special effects, on which so much time and attention were lavished, are still powerful. *Thief* remains *the* seminal large-scale film fantasy, and is completely disturbing on both the conscious and unconscious level, as mythology should be.

The story lags, the transitions are clumsy, and the dialogue is occasionally campy, but the intent—to combine available technology, unlimited imagination, and a substantial budget to create a captivating dream for adults and children—is fully realized. That dream stands ready to be dreamt again, with all its power intact more than fifty years after its creation.

Tom Horn

Elegiac western **:ATTITUDE**
Quiet, thoughtful western **:MOOD**

DIRECTOR: William Wiard (1980—U.S.A.)
CAST: Steve McQueen, Richard Farnsworth, Linda Evans
IN ENGLISH; COLOR

Montana author (*Nothing but Blue Skies*) and film director (*92 in the Shade*, see page 113) Thomas Mc-Guane wrote his finest screenplay as an elegy for the

Steve McQueen in *Tom Horn*

closing of the American West. Steve McQueen's subtle, multilayered performance is his epitaph for himself as the quintessential outrider who could not or would not conform.

Looking back on McQueen's career, there aren't that many enduring films or performances of any depth: *Bullitt* and *The Thomas Crown Affair* are vehicles, not dramas; *The Great Escape* is beyond category; except for *Hell Is for Heroes*, McQueen never really acted. He permitted the world, for the price of admission, to partake of his compelling, indifferent cool. Here, McQueen creates a character. That the character might share McQueen's world-weary love of life is no accident. McQueen plays Tom Horn with the rueful dignity of accepted doom. He plays Horn like a man who realizes that all his life's learnings will offer no assistance in coping with the modern world. (McQueen died of cancer less than three years after *Tom Horn* was released.)

Tom Horn is based on a frontier autobiography written in jail while its author awaited the hangman. . . . McQueen plays a legendary scout and gun-for-hire, who assassinates rustlers for a powerful clique of increasingly corporate, increasingly urban, Wyoming ranchers. When the ranchers recognize that bad public relations might do them more harm than rustling, they abandon Tom Horn—who is too much of the frontier to understand these new and fatal city ways. Horn is unjustly convicted of a murder he probably didn't commit—though he committed plenty of others.

Only McGuane and McQueen could make such morally ambiguous material seem such a tragedy: McGuane by eschewing his trademark excess of irony; McQueen by understating as only a true star with his entire career behind him could find the courage to do.

After a somewhat confused beginning, western action abounds, from horseback chases (McQueen's horse is amazing) to shoot-outs to lingering kisses under the golden Western sky. The casting of Linda Evans as Horn's love interest is jarring, but even she does her best work.

Tom Horn takes place during that narrow and neglected time-slice between the Old West and the new, where only the finest westerns dare tread. McGuane captures the self-conscious mythmaking that plagued everyone living in that legendary space. The ranchers eat lobster trained-in from Maine, the marshall brags about being offered a job by Buffalo Bill, and the schoolmarm refers to herself as "an adventuress." From McGuane's rhythms and dialogue grow the ever-increasing sense that his western may come nearest to capturing what the Old West was really like.

The pace is a bit erratic and the score can be overbearing, but the mood holds throughout. McQueen is hypnotizing, and the finale is extraordinarily effective and thought-provoking. A rare piece: the western that delivers all the expected western thrills, and still comments accurately and with insight on both westerns and the West, itself.

Other recommended rentals starring Steve McQueen:

Bullitt

The Great Escape

Hell Is for Heroes (see page 56)

Two-Lane Blacktop

Arty road movie **:ATTITUDE**
Drag races, blank stares, drag races **:MOOD**

DIRECTOR: Monte Hellman (1971—U.S.A.)
CAST: Warren Oates, James Taylor, Dennis Wilson, Laurie Byrd
IN ENGLISH; COLOR

Once even the screenplay for *Two-Lane Blacktop* evoked gasps of admiration—it was featured on the cover of *Esquire*—and later, gasps of horror: The movie bombed and *Esquire* called it one of the worst films of the year. Well, *Esquire* was wrong both times. It's neither a classic nor a stinkeroo, but an eccentric, self-conscious commentary on the youth culture of the early 1970s in the form of a road movie. To deliver both a satisfying road movie and insightful commentary is a tall order. Being the perverse, contradictory but irresistible piece that it is, *Two-Lane* fails and succeeds in both departments, continuously.

Monte Hellman—director of such little-known, snail-paced classics as the mock–spaghetti western *China 9, Liberty 37*—assumed the career-long role of an American middlebrow Antonioni: smart enough to realize that something profound happens when you slow the story down, but not creative enough to do much more than that.

Two-Lane, the apotheosis of Hellman's one-trick-pony technique, runs on a plot of Antonionian simplicity. Two guys share ownership of a custom hot rod—Dennis Wilson, the late drummer for the Beach Boys, and James Taylor—and cruise aimlessly around America accepting drag-race challenges for money. Taylor drives, Wilson works on the car. That's it. They seldom speak, they show no emotions, they have no names. The credits list them as "Driver" and "Mechanic."

Into their wandering midst falls model Laurie Byrd ("Girl"). Her acting is so terrible as to suggest a commentary on acting—part of Hellman's renowned, and extremely irritating, ironist's sensibility. With the arrival of Byrd, passions arise. She seduces "Driver" and then "Mechanic." While coping with this new drama, the trio meet Warren Oates, a square from Squaresville in polyester, but a drag-racing wanderer like themselves. Oates drives a Pontiac GTO; his name on the credits—"GTO."

While Wilson, Taylor, and Byrd distrust words, and connect to their own sensations and urges with unself-conscious ease. Oates is garrulous, middle-aged neurosis come to life. He's both the trio's absolute opposite and their secret brethren; an older, lamer version of themselves. Denying this unspoken connection in a rage of competition, Oates and the guys agree to a cross-country race.

They spend the rest of the movie hauling ass down an ever-narrowing succession of country roads until the finale, when everyone achieves mythic status and Hellman proves that Antonioni didn't have *all* the good ideas. No film in history ends as *Two-Lane Blacktop* ends. No other film. Ever.

Despite his attempts at commentary on road pictures, Hellman still delivers the virtues of the genre: lots of driving, lots of quiet landscapes, a little sex, and several admirable cars.

Think of a European art film on a subject no European really understands (except Wim Wenders), starring actors whose archetypal Americanness is the very reason they were cast. The potency of these seeming contradictions forms only a fraction of the picture's peculiar, enduring power. If you can adjust to the glacial pace, you will be spellbound and ultimately rewarded.

Vanishing Point

Dope-fueled road movie :**ATTITUDE**
Car chases, hippie philosophizing, car chases :**MOOD**

DIRECTOR: Richard Sarafian (1971—U.S.A.)
CAST: Barry Newman, Severn Darden, Cleavon Little
IN ENGLISH; COLOR

The joys of road movies are the joys of the road; the point's not the getting there but the going. A major-league snootful of marijuana may or may not help the drive, but it certainly seems to have fueled this absolute classic of an art form as purely American as jazz or the western. *Vanishing Point* is the ultimate road movie: There's not the slightest purpose to it, only the road.

Barry Newman plays a guy with a head full of Benzedrine and a heart full of obsession. He wants to drive and never stop. Commitment, love, conversation, cops, speed limits—that's all too plastic, man! Barry seeks the uncut salvation of speed. In pursuit of that obsession he accepts a bet to take a car—which, fortunately for him, turns out to be a hemihead Challenger: a serious muscle machine—from Denver to San Francisco in fifteen hours, a definitive hauling of butt.

Barry hits the road with only his envelope of amphetamines, but since road movies are by definition buddy pictures, Barry needs a buddy. And since Barry's in his car all day (and all night and all day again), the only relationship he's capable of sustaining is with his radio. And thence his buddy emerges, a black, blind DJ named, shamelessly enough, Super Soul—maniacally portrayed by Cleavon Little.

Super Soul clues into Barry's mad ride by listening to police-band radios—the cops are chasing Barry for speeding—and communicates with Barry via pronouncements over the air. Barry talks back to the radio and, though Super Soul can't hear him in his radio station a hundred miles away, he answers Barry *as if he really could!* It's like , cosmic. Super Soul and Barry, communicating via the spheres, form a genuine and moving bond.

While the pacing and direction of any scene not having to do with driving is scattered, not to say aimless, cinematographer John Alonzo does wonders with the wide-open spaces. He knows a million different ways to shoot the inside and outside of speeding cars. All of them are entertaining.

Barry meets some engaging archetypes on the road, as all picaresque heroes must. Seventies character-actor stalwarts Dean Jagger, Severn Darden (are there any dope-fueled, worthy trash films from the 1970s that *don't* feature Severn Darden?), and Paul Koslo appear. Koslo plays a particularly determined cop with that nice, frothing-at-the-mouth psychotic undertone he brings to all his performances.

There is little dialogue and less plot development. But the true mood of the road—of elegiac sadness; of endless potential and no payoff; of the momentary brotherhood between those who race; of bitterness washed away in a constant reaching for the horizon; in short, of the irresistible romance of the highway—is evoked with a purity, longing, and sweetness that have no equal in the genre. Director Richard Sarafian also understood how all road trips must come to an end.

A film you may not watch as much as experience, and one that will surprise you with the strength of its pull. Stirring and memorable all out of proportion to its budget or to the quality of its execution.

Vernon, Florida

The real "Twin Peaks" :ATTITUDE
Profoundly strange documentary :MOOD

DIRECTOR: Errol Morris (1980—U.S.A.)
IN ENGLISH; COLOR

As with *Gates of Heaven* (see page 53), Errol Morris went on location thinking he would make a film on one subject, but ended up shooting another. Morris was initially drawn to the town of Vernon, Florida, by its fame in the insurance business. Vernon, known by insurers as "Nub City," had the highest per capita incidence of self-mutilation, for the purpose of faking accidents and thereby collecting insurance payments, of any town in America. Or so Morris claimed.

He intended to film those who had wrecked their bodies for monetary gain, but found instead a town of such surpassing strangeness that he settled for a simple, powerful portrait of the inhabitants. The film consists of people talking to the camera, nothing more. The director's voice is never heard, no questions are asked and Morris encourages his subjects to talk on and on. At first it's maddening, then hypnotic, then, as comprehension dawns, inspiring.

Morris is imbued with a patience few documentarians possess. If he holds his shots long enough, he believes, his subjects will strip themselves bare. And they always do, confessing to Morris the most horrible corners of their hearts, sometimes by accident, sometimes with full and grim self-congratulation. To enjoy this sort of hyper-realism, one must relax into Morris's extended sense of time, to accept that the drama lies in the contradiction between the endless takes and static frames, and the psychic violence of his subject's confessions. In the most quiet, apparently boring moments, they say the most appalling things.

The framing is slightly off-kilter and the colors are rich, reminiscent of the still photographs of William Eggleston. The editing is stately, metronomic, and always in sync with the pace of the confessions. And, as in *Gates,* the sum of the confessing adds up to way more than the whole of its parts.

Once again, he has induced the simplest folk to take on the most complex questions. His subjects serve as metaphors for his own bleak worldview and abiding sense of hopelessness and dread. Their dead-end lives are worthy of preservation, Morris seems to contend, because they mirror our own lives, which are no less devoid of meaning. If we believe these (inarticulate, rural, undereducated) people are more destitute of insight than we, we are in error.

No matter whether we meet a turkey-hunting obsessive, a man with a captive raccoon, or a couple who treasure their collection of sand because they are convinced it grows daily (!), they all talk about the purpose of existence and how they recognize that their lives are slipping by. All discuss in some fashion their perception of their place in the universe. All experience guilt over some misdeed, or work hard to pretend that they've never experienced such a thing.

When one Vernonian pulls his captive raccoon out of a barrel and holds it just above the sandy soil, the animal reaches out with his front paws and makes several feeble scratches, into the ground. The man drops it back in the barrel. Morris swings the camera away from him, zooms in on the scratches, and holds the shot for an interminable length of time. It seems that even the animals of Vernon provide Morris with a metaphor for the pointlessness, brevity, and transitory nature of our efforts on this earth.

Though this sounds unremittingly bleak—hey, it *is* unremittingly bleak—it's also compellingly weird and very funny. However unnerving Morris's deadpan presentation of the American underbelly may be, his utterly committed yet never exploitative approach grants it profundity.

Other recommended rentals directed by Errol Morris:
A Brief History of Time
Gates of Heaven (see page 53)
The Thin Blue Line

Voyager

> *Accursed synchronicity* **:ATTITUDE**
> *Slow, heartbreaking drama* **:MOOD**

DIRECTOR: Volker Schlöndorff (1992—U.S.A.)
CAST: Sam Shepard, Julie Delpy, Barbara Sukowa
IN ENGLISH; COLOR

Among the saddest films ever made; a treatise on fate, synchronicity, self-knowledge, denial, and love.

Director Schlöndorff, seeking to counterbalance the tragedy of the plot, composes for maximum loveliness and casts the most striking actors: Sam Shepard, Julie Delpy, and Barbara Sukowa. All are clad in the best Armani and lit with softened sunlight. Placed against the backdrop of the Mexican desert, the deep blue ocean, the gardens of Paris, and the ruins of Rome, Schlöndorff presents these golden idols as living charmed lives. When we believe it as completely as they, Schlöndorff lowers the boom.

Sam Shepard plays a super-American of the 1950s, a world-builder, an unemotional engineer (when his plane begins to crash, Shepard pulls out his slide rule to calculate their exact rate of descent). When his plane crash-lands in the desert, coincidence returns him to his once best friend, a man who married Shepard's most significant ex-girlfriend (Barbara Sukowa). When Shepard goes to meet his old friend—whom he has not seen in twenty years—he discovers the man has committed suicide. It's the first link in a chain of coincidence that will destroy Shepard's life. Or, if you prefer, it's the first step that Shepard takes toward reaping that which he has sown.

Shepard sails on an ocean liner to Europe. On board he meets a beautiful young girl played by Julie Delpy. He courts her awkwardly, as if unaware of the depth of his attraction to her. He insists on driving her from Paris to Athens. Shepard shirks a professional responsibility to do so, and is amazed at his uncharacteristic willfulness. He and the girl become lovers.

To his horror, he learns that Julie Delpy's mother is his old girlfriend and that his old friend who committed suicide is the girl's father. He does not tell the girl about her father. As they near Athens, Shepard's apprehension grows; how will he explain to his old girlfriend that he is now her daughter's lover? How will he tell his old girlfriend of her ex-husband's suicide? Entangling his emotions even more are his memories of the former girlfriend: how he felt betrayed by her, and her by him. Shepard's caught on the wheel of fate, and fate ain't done with him; there's a defining tragedy yet to be endured.

Director Schlöndorff is no Stanley Kubrick; he has compassion for all his characters. He villainizes no one, and everyone's pain is painfully clear. Adapted from the novel *Homo Faber* ("Man the Maker"), Schlöndorff's screenplay takes a grim view of man's efforts, and depicts a universe determined to undo hopes and dreams. Schlöndorff's care in re-creating the novel only makes its message that much harder to refute.

Shepard sets the tone with his conversational rhythms and toned-down manner. Julie Delpy rose to stardom on her bloom-of-youth radiance, and she's at her most lovely. Barbara Sukowa's character is driven by a willful, hardheaded spitefulness. Her scenes with Shepard are wrenching in their honesty, and in the accuracy of their depiction of old lovers reviving twenty years' worth of bitterness.

Not an optimistic view of things, to say the least. Slow, in that non-commital German way, with no plot or character aspect fully explained nor completely mysterious. A film for adults, as uncynical and true a depiction of loss as you will ever see.

Other recommended rentals directed by Volker Schlöndorff:
Circle of Deceit

Who'll Stop the Rain?

American psychosis :**ATTITUDE**
Profound, violent, chase movie :**MOOD**

DIRECTOR: Karel Reisz (1978—U.S.A.)
CAST: Nick Nolte, Tuesday Weld, Richard Masur, Anthony Zerbe
IN ENGLISH; COLOR

Reviled by the studio that produced it, forgotten the day after
it opened, no movie says more
about America after Vietnam.

The calm, distanced tone
and dispassionate visuals belie
the profundity of the screenplay, which the director
adapted with remarkable sensitivity from the novel *Dog
Soldiers* by author Robert
Stone. Nobody chronicles the
American spiritual/moral rot-
from-within like Stone. His
métier is the poisonous stew
of self-interest, folly, and good
intentions that marks American foreign affairs, drug poli-

Nick Nolte and Riachard Masur in
Who'll Stop the Rain?

cies, and law enforcement. Presenting Stone's view with admirable
fealty to the book, director Reisz's vision proved too nihilistic to succeed at the box office.

It's not that Reisz (or, heaven forbid, Stone) strives to be inaccessible; both recognize that no American audience would tolerate profound tragedy without chase scenes, shoot-outs, or antiheroes, and
they supply only the best. And despite its brutal violence and de-

pressing "message," *Rain* is, in its own graveyard hipster fashion, surprisingly funny.

Michael Moriarty plays a journalist rendered a moral wreck by his experiences covering the war in Vietnam. He enlists a psycho veteran who thinks of himself as a Nietzschean Zen Samurai (Nick Nolte) to help smuggle "a shitload of heroin" from 'Nam to the States. Being amateurs, they run afoul of the corrupt law enforcement conspiracy that masterminded the smuggling, with Moriarty as its unknowing dupe.

Nolte flees the crooked cops with Moriarty's wife, played to neurotic perfection by Tuesday Weld, and together they run from San Francisco to Los Angeles to New Mexico. Their journey takes them through every imaginable permutation of the postwar, postcounterculture culture: rich weirdos, aging commies, Hollywood heroin dealers, and abandoned communes, all detailed with cruel wit and insight.

Moriarty, held hostage by those hunting his wife, travels as a prisoner in a netherworld of stoolies-turned-cops and armed junkies–turned–dope trackers. Moriarty and his escort of killers catch up to Nolte and Weld on the Mexican borderline. Struggling for possession of the heroin, they allegorically enact the End of the Sixties. The existential metaphors fly as thick and fast as bullets from an M-16. Those fly, also.

Moriarty shows little emotion, his blank face and calm voice suit his character's malaise. Nolte, then unknown, brings compassionate insight to a guy whose constant posing masks his pathetic, if homicidal, sincerity. Tuesday Weld acts like an adult for once. Either her role or the circumstances of performing it produce an all-too-believable edge of insanity. She's perfect.

The wondrous supporting cast includes Anthony Zerbe as an evil D.A.; Ray Sharkey, crazy as ever as a junkie hit man; Richard Masur as a chess-playing torturer, and, creating one of the memorable slimeballs in cinema history, Charles Haid (*Hill Street Blues*) as the indescribably corrupt, and unintentionally hilarious, Hollywood dope dealer, Eddie.

The realism of these extraordinary characters springs from their eccentric dialogue, which Stone wrote and which Reisz leaves wholly intact. Reisz devotes himself to staying out of the way; his visual style is unobtrusive and he focuses on his actors, none of whom were ever better. The producing studio, unwilling to name the film after the book, titled it after the best-known song on a quirky but well-chosen sound track.

It feels like an art movie, but it's funny; it's deep and philosophical, but folks get shot; it's clearly a morality tale, but there ain't no moral.

It's the anti-*Gump* incarnate.

The Wild Angels

Biker movie **:ATTITUDE**
Leather jackets, go-go boots, and cool bikes **:MOOD**

DIRECTOR: Roger Corman (1966—U.S.A.)
CAST: Peter Fonda, Nancy Sinatra, Bruce Dern
IN ENGLISH; COLOR

Nancy Sinatra, Diane Ladd, Peter Fonda, and the Venice, CA, Hell's Angels in *The Wild Angels*

Turned into outcasts by a hypocritical, oppressive society, bikers believe that there's nothing to believe in, and they believe it with all their hearts. In a world unworthy of faith, they have faith only in the world they make, in loyalty to one another, in being cool, and in the transitory freedom of the open road. At least that's the morality code that movie bikers exemplified during the brief, wonderful mid-1960s reign of the biker film as a drive-in movie exploitation genre.

Easy Rider both culminated and destroyed the biker film. Before it, biker films had suggested a brothers-under-the-skin affinity between real bikers (working-class rebels) and the emerging hippie culture (middle-class rebels). That idea seemed rather naive after Altamont. . . .

Easy Rider furthered the redneck-hippie polarization, creating an us-against-them climate in which no movie dared glamorize inherently antihippie bikers. Emerging four years prior to *Easy Rider,* when most of America had never even *seen* a hippie, *The Wild Angels* avoids the subject altogether. It's the most inward-looking, biker-culture obsessed, and hard-core of all biker movies. It presents biker life as a desperate, dead-end, but not inconceivable response to plastic, conformist "Amerika."

The Wild Angels prefigures *Easy Rider* in a number of ways, not least that Peter Fonda stars in both as the archetypal sensitive-guy biker (as opposed to the reactive thug-biker of Dennis Hopper in *Easy Rider* and Bruce Dern in *The Wild Angels).* Both films feature the best-designed bikes and biker clothing. While the sound track for *Easy Rider* proved for the first time that hippie rock 'n' roll could fuel a movie (and find a paying audience), the sound track for *The Wild Angels* is a typically pathetic collection of mock-Ventures twangy guitars and anemic pop. Still, the theme song rocks.

Peter Fonda plays Blue, a biker at a lifestyle crossroads. His girl-friend—Nancy Sinatra in go-go boots, miniskirt, push-up bra, and ironed hair—clings to Peter in supportive awe at his laid-back sensitivity. Bruce Dern plays Fonda's hotheaded pal, who loses his job, steals a bike, and is shot by a motorcycle cop during an extended chase sequence. Dern's funeral—staged according to accounts of a Hell's Angels funeral, reported by Hunter S. Thompson in *Esquire*—proves a wild bacchanal. A church is destroyed, a priest punched out, the corpse propped up in his coffin with a joint in his mouth, the dead man's girlfriend ritualistically raped by his own biker pals, and several citizens assaulted. The funeral ends with a dramatic procession of hungover, unrepentant bikers, which includes members of the Venice, California, chapter of the Hell's Angels.

Fonda buries Dern and, as the cops descend to wreak vengeance, refuses to run away. "Nothing to say," are his rueful final words as he stands next to the grave, shovel in hand, awaiting the hard justice about to befall him. Fonda perceives that biker culture, when it succumbs to the excesses of the larger society, is every bit as bankrupt. Rebelling against rebellion, he has, in his own words, "Nowhere to go." Fonda gave his all for a world he believed in. What remains for him now that he has no faith?

It's a hell of a statement, a tightrope of oxymorons: Corman both romanticizes the biker life and finds it bereft of worth. Corman understood antiheroes like nobody's business; does he present such nihilism as a commercial gambit or does he really find the biker/outlaw culture unredeemable? Either way, the image of Fonda staring down at the grave, confused and defiant but ready to be punished, served as the antiestablishment behavioral model until those *Easy Rider* rednecks blew him off his chopper four years later. . . .

Other recommended biker-movie rentals:
Hell's Angels on Wheels (directed by Richard Rush)
The Savage Seven (Richard Rush)

Withnail and I

End of the sixties :ATTITUDE
Nasty, dope-fueled English comedy :MOOD

DIRECTOR: Bruce Robinson (1986—U.K.)
CAST: Richard E. Grant, Paul McGann, Richard Griffiths, Ralph Brown
IN ENGLISH; COLOR

A very English, eccentric, much-loved comedy of choosing life over decay, set in swinging London, circa 1969. The party's winding down, and dues must be paid. . . .

In this misanthropic masterpiece, writer-director Bruce Robinson (screenwriter of *The Killing Fields*) vents his spleen through the character of Withnail (Richard E. Grant in the role he was born to play), a resolutely unemployed actor from a crippling upper-class background. Withnail prides himself on the strength of his refusal to participate in the world, and on his dissolution. He drinks whatever he can lay his hands on—including aftershave—and dares his dope dealer to waste him. "I'll take anything you've got," Withnail tells his dealer, "and run a mile."

Withnail's pal and roommate, identified only as "I," is another unemployed long-haired actor. He drinks and dopes slightly less than Withnail, and actually leaves the house in search of acting jobs. Withnail has long since given up. He's waiting for the world to come to his door, and the efforts of others move him to withering scorn. "I" faces Withnail's contempt whenever he speaks an optimistic or conciliatory thought.

Desperate to escape their miserable apartment where the dirty dishes are linked by months of mold, they flee to the rural cottage of Withnail's Uncle Monty. After a series of misadventures resulting from their helpless urban ways, Monty shows up to rescue them. He brings fine wines, a lavish dinner, and misplaced carnal intentions. Later that night—wrongly convinced that "I" is Withnail's lover—Monty chases "I" throughout the cottage. "I" and Withnail escape Monty and return, dispirited, to their dreary flat (so cold that they rub the English equivalent of Vicks VaporRub all over themselves to get warm).

"I" finds a small job in a regional theater (just the sort of work most likely to raise Withnail's ire), cuts his hair (a gesture certain to evoke Withnail's most wounding disdain), and prepares to leave the 1960s, self-destruction, and Withnail himself, behind.

Withnail may be anarchy made flesh, but there's nothing anarchic about Robinson's screenplay. He's a master of structure and understatement. Robinson shoots in dark, somber colors, the tones of a rainy English winter, and directs his actors within a tightly composed frame. The story is carried by the dialogue, and so Robinson's technique provides a calm foundation for continual, delirious conversation.

Scathing attacks are Withnail's area of specialization. Despite his nastiness, his cowardice, his love of laying blame, and his tragic willingness to let his life go to hell, Withnail remains undeniably charismatic. The drunker he gets, the more savagely articulate he becomes. And the more bile he pours out, the clearer it is that Withnail hates others only a tiny bit less than he hates himself. Thus revealed, his wasted life is not funny, but tragic.

Nonstop, breathtakingly articulate wordplay; characters you know from life but have never seen before on the screen; dialogue you will repeat to your friends for months; and the least stupid dope jokes you ever heard.

Other recommended rentals directed by Bruce Robinson:
How to Get Ahead in Advertising

As comprehensive as I hoped this book to be, some wonderful movies remain unavailable in any home-video format. So, after you've rented all the films herein, pester your video store until they come up with:

The Big Carnival aka **Ace in the Hole** (1961—U.S.A, directed by Billy Wilder)

The Great Ecstacy of the Sculptor Steiner (1975—Germany, directed by Werner Herzog)

I Walked with a Zombie (1943—USA, directed by Jaques Tourneur)

La Maman et la Putain (1973—France, directed by Jean Eustache)

Los Olvidados (1950—Mexico, directed by Luis Bunuel)

Radio On (1980—England, directed by Christopher Petit)

Walkabout (1970—Australia, directed by Nicolas Roeg

RENTING & PURCHASING MOVIES BY MAIL AND THE INTERNET

■ If you live in New York City, you can rent the most obscure film in this book by strolling a few blocks to one of many art-movie video shops. But what if you live in a more remote outpost of America, Ketchum, Idaho, say? How can you rent these films?

Surprisingly, many of the 100 Best Films are available at any regular video outlet, at least those pictures distributed by major studios. For foreign, independent, and classic films, there are several worthy options for renting by mail. There are even more options for purchasing tapes or laser discs.

Mail-order rental houses print catalogs, for which they charge, or they offer memberships. Catalog houses mail regular updates to subscribers and offer 800 numbers for requesting a specific title. Their rental fees can be as much as $10 per film—but these fees allow you to keep a mail-order movie for three days. Your rental fee includes return postage and tapes are sent in a reusable mailer-boxes with prepaid labels. All rental catalogues require a credit-card deposit. The folks at the mail-order houses are quite friendly and helpful. While each of the catalogs listed below strives to be comprehensive, if you subscribe to all three you should be able to find any film currently available on video.

The Internet is an excellent source of sources. You can find several videotape and laser-disc sales houses by calling up any search engine, such as Yahoo, Alta Vista, or Webcrawler, and typing in "laser disc" or "video."

RENTAL CATALOGS

Video Library 1-800-669-7157

Home Film Festival 1-800-258-3456

Facets Video 1-800-532-2387

VIDEO AND LASER-DISC PURCHASE

Ken Crane's Laserdisc 1-800-624-3078

Scarecrow Video 1-800-700-8554

Laser Perceptions 1-415-753-2016

WEB SITES

Powernet Video Rental
   http://www.pwrnet.com/MALL/VIDEOSTORE/order.html
Teen Movie Critic's List of Video Rental Stores by State
   http://www.dreamagic.com/roger/videostores/states0.html
Forum Video Online
   http://www.forumvideo.com/index.html

RECOMMENDED READING

Bandy, Mary Lee. *Rediscovering French Film*. New York: Museum of Modern Art, 1983.

Bluestone, George. *Novels into Film: The Metamorphosis of Fiction into Cinema*. Berkeley, CA: University of California Press, 1957.

Bobker, Lee R. *Elements of Film*. New York: Harcourt, Brace & World, 1969.

Bondanella, Peter. *Italian Cinema from Neo-Realism to the Present*. New York: Frederick Ungar Publishing, 1983.

Brown, Royal S. *Focus on Godard*. Englewood Cliffs, NJ: Prentice-Hall International, 1972.

Christie, Ian. *Arrows of Desire: The Films of Michael Powell and Emeric Pressburger*. London: Faber and Faber, 1985.

Copjec, Joan. *Shades of Noir*. London, England: Verso, 1993.

Cowie, Peter. *The Cinema of Orson Welles*. New York: Da Capo Press, 1993.

Crenshaw, Marshall. *Hollywood Rock*. New York: Harper Perennial, 1994.

Dymtryk, Edward. *On Film Editing*. Boston: Focal Press, 1984.

Haskell, Molly. *From Reverence to Rape: The Treatment of Women in the Movies*. Chicago: University of Chicago Press, 1987.

Hillier, Jim. *Cahiers du Cinéma, The 1950s: Neo-Realism, Hollywood, New Wave*. Cambridge, MA: Harvard University Press, 1985.

———. *Cahiers du Cinéma, The 1960s: New Wave, New Cinema, Reevaluating Hollywood*. Cambridge, MA: Harvard University Press, 1985.

Kael, Pauline. *Kiss Kiss Bang Bang*. New York: Bantam Books, 1968.

———. *For Keeps: 30 Years at the Movies*. New York: Dutton, 1984.

Katz, Ephraim. *The Film Encyclopedia*. New York: HarperCollins, 1994.

Katz, Stephen D. *Film Directing Shot by Shot*. Studio City, CA: Michael Wiese Productions, 1991.

Kolker, Robert and Peter Beichen. *The Films of Wim Wenders: Cinema As Vision and Despair*. New York: Cambridge Press, 1993.

Krutnik, Frank. *In a Lonely Place: Film Noir, Genre, Masculinity*. London: Routledge, 1991.

Mamet, David. *On Directing Film.* New York: Penguin Books, 1991.

Marcus, Millicent. *Italian Film in the Light of Neorealism.* Princeton, NJ: Princeton University Press, 1986.

Milne, Tom. *Godard on Godard.* New York: Viking Press, 1992.

Nelson, Thomas Allen. *Kubrick: Inside a Film Artist's Maze.* Bloomington, ID: University of Indiana Press, 1982.

Melville, Jean-Pierre. *Melville on Melville.* Edited by Rue Noruiega. New York: Viking Press, 1971.

Peary, Danny. *Guide for the Film Fanatic.* New York: Fireside Books, 1986.

———. *Cult Movies 3.* New York: Fireside Books, 1988.

———. *Cult Movie Stars.* New York: Fireside Books, 1991.

Place, J.A. *The Western Films of John Ford.* Secaucus, NJ: Citadel Press, 1974.

Powell, Michael. *Edge of the World: The Making of a Film.* London: Faber and Faber, 1938.

———. *Million Dollar Movie.* New York: Random House, 1992.

Rafferty, Terrence. *The Thing Happens: Ten Years of Writing About the Movies.* New York: Grove Press, 1995.

Roud, Richard. *Cinema, A Critical Dictionary: The Major Film-Makers.* New York: Viking Press, 1980.

Silver, Alain and Elizabeth Ward. *Film Noir: An Encyclopedic Reference to the American Style.* Woodstock, NY: Overlook Press, 1979.

Sklar, Robert. *Movie-Made America.* New York: Vintage, 1976.

———. *Film: An International History of the Medium.* New York: Harry N. Abrams, 1993.

Time Out Editors. *The Time Out Film Guide,* 4th ed. London: Penguin Press, 1995.

Vale, V. and Andre Juno. *Incredibly Strange Films.* San Francisco: RE/Search Publications, 1986.

Wenders, Wim. *Emotion Pictures.* London: Faber and Faber, 1994.

ACKNOWLEDGMENTS

■ Many thanks to my parents, Anne and Sylvan Meyer of Miami Beach, Florida, and Dahlonega, Georgia, for their love and support.

Thanks to Heather Jackson, my editor at St. Martin's Press, for her commitment to this book, enthusiasm, humor, and for her great taste in movies.

Thanks to Michael and Celeste Earles of *Sun Valley Magazine*, for their support and nurturing of my column, "The Ten Best Films to Rent You Never Heard Of," which formed the genesis of this book.

Michael Schulman and everyone at Archive found the great photos reprinted here, and proved themselves saints of patience, thoroughness, and good judgement.

Namasté to my soulmates Diane Crist, Rick Slone, and Stella Keane of Ketchum, Idaho, and Tim Bailey, wherever he may be. Their loving kindness and support enabled me to believe in myself and in my work.

Others in Ketchum whose friendship encouraged me to write this book include: Michael and Ruthann Saphier, Sheryl (and everyone) at *Chapter One*, Suzy from *Main Street Bookcafe*, Marguerite (Davis) Wilkens, Anette Farnham, Deborah Brammer, Michael Medberry, and Laird Erman.

Thanks also to Sally Brock and Marcelle Pearson at *The Sun Valley Center for the Arts and Humanities*, and to all my film students there, especially the Bishoffs, Millie Wiggins, Jan Cox, and Alison White. Thanks also to Libby Sullivan for her astute commentary.

In New York, thanks to Julie Peters, Nancy Hass, and to my community at Cinemax/HBO: Marilyn McAleer, Mark Davidson, Geoff Bird, Susan Walker, and Katherine Jewell.

And hey, what about that Judy Fox? Whatta gal!

Thanks to my rock of encouragement, old friend, and email companion, Julie Ardery, for her enthusiasm, constancy, and faith. Kim Howard of Hailey, Idaho, shared her inspirational optimism and gave me the best advice any writer could receive. Thank you, Kim.

My greatest debt of gratitude and heartfelt thanks are owed to Cristina Seckinger. I could not have written this book without her generous love, trust, and care.

DIRECTORS

ACTORS

RENTAL CATEGORY